Parent-Friendly Early Learning

Tips and Strategies for Working Well with Families

Julie Powers

Redleaf Press
St. Paul, Minnesota
www.redleafpress.org

Published by Redleaf Press
a division of Resources for Child Caring
10 Yorkton Court
St. Paul, MN 55117
Visit us online at www.redleafpress.org.

Cover design by Amy Kirkpatrick
Interior design by Eric Vollen

Redleaf Press books are available at a special discount when purchased in bulk for special premiums and sales promotions. For details, contact the sales manager at 800-423-8309.

Library of Congress Cataloging-in-Publication Data

Powers, Julie, 1957–
    Parent-friendly early learning : tips and strategies for working well with families / Julie Powers.
        p. cm.
    Includes bibliographical references.
    ISBN:10 1-929610-62-9 (pbk.)
    ISBN:13 978-1-929610-62-4
    1. Early childhood education—Parent participation. 2. Parent-teacher relationships. I. Title.
LB1139.35.P37P693 2005
372.21—dc22

                                                                    2004029619

Manufactured in the United States of America

12 11 10 09 08 07 06 05   1 2 3 4 5 6 7 8

For Marty Rosenthal,
who encouraged and supported me
through completion of this book,

Gabriel Powers,
who was patient while I learned how to be a parent,

Maggie Bryson,
one of the best teachers we ever lost,

and Kathy Kolb,
who understood my intent and helped me find
the book inside me.

Contents

Acknowledgments

Thanks to the following:

Marjorie Schiller, who always thinks I am smarter than I am

Eva Moravcik, who trusted my ego with her mighty red pen and made improvements to this book

Roger and Bonnie Neugebauer, who believed I had something to say to my colleagues

Stephanie Feeney, who taught me how to think about professional ethics

Margarita Kay, who taught me to look at cultural context

Betty Jones, who pushed me to improve my writing

Nancy Burrows, who modeled the role teachers can play in improving parent competency

Kay Rencken, who helped me find my professional voice

Nancy Sergeant-Abbate, who taught me how to collaborate with parents

Beth Wallace, who stepped in at the eleventh hour and saw to it that this book was the best it could be

Marcie Oltman, Jenny Hanlon, Natalie Dube, Louie Kolberg, Sarah Sivright, Sheila Williams-Ridge, Kathy Zampier, Susan Knutson, Joel Creswell, Jacky Turchick, Rheta Kuwahara, Cheryl Takashige, and Doug Rowe for sharing their stories of working with families

All of the families of University of Hawaii at Manoa Children's Center, Dodge Nature Preschool, Valley View Preschool, and Tucson Community School for sharing their children with me

Introduction

Have you ever worked with a teacher who thrives on working with parents? For some teachers, relationships with parents are as fulfilling as relationships with children. Rather than stressing out before parent-teacher conferences, they look forward to the time they will spend talking about the children. Parents seem to listen to their advice and trust them with family issues. These teachers are even able to tell parents hard truths without being met with defensiveness. Are they just natural parent-educators? Some may be. Others may have been uncomfortable working with parents and learned to enjoy this aspect of their work as they gained skills in building relationships with parents. If you find working with parents one of the more difficult aspects of your job, you are not alone. This book will help you understand how teachers develop those "natural" relationships with parents and teach you the skills you need to enjoy your work with families.

One of the critical keys to working well with parents is learning to see their perspective. Many parents share similar perspectives about rearing children and interacting with the teachers who care for them. We can appreciate children for who they are and take pleasure in their company when we understand their development and their unique way of looking at the world. We enjoy some children more than others, even if we pretend we like them all the same, but as teachers we know how to make relationships with all children. The same can be true for parents. They are unique individuals and we will enjoy some more than others, but we can create relationships with all of them. Sometimes the parents who are challenging end up being the parents we feel the closest bond to. Working with parents makes teaching more satisfying and affects the entire family as well as making us better professionals.

Why Is It Important for Us to Work with Families?

It is possible to see the need to work well with parents as just one more demand on teachers. Aren't children the most important focus of our work? Why should we dilute our efforts and focus on parents as well?

❋ **We have a lot to offer parents.**
As early childhood professionals, we have special insight into young children. We can help parents differentiate between issues that are related to general development and issues that are individual for their children. We can help them keep their expectations age appropriate and offer solutions to struggles they are having with their children.

❋ **Parents have a lot to offer us.**
Parents know their children well—and they can help us find strategies to best teach their children. They know best how to read their children's feelings and what are their children's preferences and abilities. Our jobs will be easier in partnership with parents.

❋ **It's the best thing for children.**
Children gain the most from the early education experience if a partnership exists between staff and families. We are in children's lives for a relatively short period of time. If we have an impact on the whole family and affect how parents interact with their children, we make a contribution that will last a lifetime.

Why Do Some Teachers Find It So Hard to Work with Parents?

Talking to parents can practically paralyze some teachers. As Shawna says, "I just dread parent-teacher conferences! I get so nervous—all of my thoughts just leave my brain! Sometimes parents get defensive if I tell them anything less than glowing about their children."

Communicating with parents can be especially hard for new teachers. Parents may not demonstrate patience with the learning curve for novice teachers. Anxious parents may cross-examine teachers or hover to make sure everything is okay. Building confidence is hard if you feel yourself being constantly critiqued.

Sometimes there is a cultural or economic divide between parents and teachers. I spoke to one teacher who moved from working with Head Start to a private, upper-income school. She said, "They treat me like I am a servant! When I was in Head Start, the parents appreciated everything I did and treated me like a professional. Now, I have these parents who expect me to wait on them and meet their personal needs."

Sometimes teachers struggle if they are not parents themselves. They may have difficulty relating to the lives and concerns of parents. These teachers may feel defensive about their judgment and advice to parents.

Some early childhood teachers just relate and interact better with children than with adults. Some of the traits that make a great early childhood educator—such as finding the behavior and personalities of children inherently interesting or having a talent for staying in the background rather than being the center of attention—do not translate to being able to socialize well with adults.

How Can We Learn to Love Working with Families?

Most of us have what it takes to be good at working with parents. The characteristics that make us good with children can also serve us in our work with parents:

❋ We know how to facilitate learning.
❋ We appreciate individual differences.
❋ We focus on development.
❋ We are warm and caring.
❋ We are willing to give others the benefit of the doubt.
❋ We enjoy the development of competency.
❋ We develop warm relationships.
❋ We can make a difference.

First, we know how to create learning opportunities that allow children to construct their own knowledge. We can do that with parents as well. By picking up on the subtle cues of readiness to find answers to what frustrates them in their work as parents, we can guide them toward finding solutions that work for their families. Our classrooms are laboratories for learning about children. When we share our insights and experiences with parents, and when we invite them into our world of the classroom, we can help them learn about their children.

Second, we accept children from wherever they are developmentally when they come to our classrooms and celebrate their quirky and unique personalities. If we can find room in our hearts to appreciate parents as individuals, they will enrich our lives. We can include their special talents and skills as we invite them into our classrooms. We can enjoy their senses of humor, be awed by their insights, and learn from them as people.

We also know how to support development, even when it is variable. We can use these same skills as we work with parents. We can work with a parent who is a genius in her own field but can't quite get herself and her child organized in the morning as well as the parent who is wonderful with his child but hasn't developed self-confidence in the decisions he makes as a parent. We can see that both of these people are still developing as parents. By paying attention to the development of parents, we can have reasonable expectations and not be disappointed when all parents don't make the choices we'd like them to make.

Teachers tend to be warm people who are comfortable with our emotions as well as the feelings of others. This characteristic helps us work well with parents who may be experiencing a merry-go-round of emotions as they learn how to parent.

We tend to be positive and optimistic people. We expect that even children who are struggling are going to turn out okay. We can use that optimism to anticipate the best in the parents we work with. We can enjoy parents. Some of the aspects of working with children we love the most can also be present when working with families.

We can tap into the joy of a parent's discovery in the same way we feel joy the first time a child pumps on a swing or writes her name. Watching a parent offer his child a choice rather than getting mad at her or overhearing one parent describe a difficult stage of their child's development they lived through can be very gratifying.

We appreciate the affection children have for us, and we grow very fond of them. Some of us cry when children leave our programs. We can also enjoy very special relationships with parents. We have shared a wonderful time in the lives of their children. We are a quiet fan club for each child, noticing his growth and achievements together. The relationships we develop with parents, whether professional or informal, can be a source of great enjoyment. As a program director, I love to listen to easy laughter coming from parents and teachers at conferences as they enjoy their shared wisdom about a particular child.

We are not a cynical group. When Sue Bredekamp gave the closing keynote speech at the 2003 National Association for the Education of Young Children (NAEYC) Conference in Chicago, she described the culture of early childhood educators. Some of what makes us who we are prepares us for enjoying our work with families. One of the most relevant aspects of our culture is our belief that we make the world a better place through our work. When we collaborate with parents to meet the needs of the children we serve, our energies and commitment have an even bigger effect on families and children.

Are You Ready to Develop Partnerships with Parents?

Attitudes and beliefs play a strong role in our ability to create partnerships. Take the following quiz to determine your own readiness.

1. Most parents want what is best for their children.
   A. True   B. Somewhat true   C. Not true

2. If parents don't agree with me, one of us does not have to be wrong.
   A. True   B. Somewhat true   C. Not true

3. Children benefit from communication and collaboration between their parents and teachers.
   A. True   B. Somewhat true   C. Not true

4. My job is more enjoyable because of my interactions with parents.
   A. True   B. Somewhat true   C. Not true

5. Parents can offer me insight about their children that will help me do a better job.
   A. True   B. Somewhat true   C. Not true

6. I can think beyond my own preferences and convenience to benefit children and parents.
   A. True   B. Somewhat true   C. Not true

7. Parents are entitled to the last say in their children's care and education.
   A. True   B. Somewhat true   C. Not true

8. I am willing to change routines and practices if it works better for children and parents.
   A. True   B. Somewhat true   C. Not true

9. I grow as a professional through interaction with parents.
   A. True   B. Somewhat true   C. Not true

How did you do? The results of your reactions to these questions lets you know how your feelings can help or hinder your relationships with parents.

* If you mostly answered *C*, you may have attitudes and beliefs that will interfere with building partnerships. Viewing parents as adversaries, problems, or a waste of your time will hold you back from making changes. As you read the following chapters, listen to the voices of parents and see if you can shift your thinking.

* If you mostly answered *B*, you demonstrate interest in creating partnerships with parents but need to keep your conflicting attitudes in mind. As you find yourself reacting negatively to the actions of parents, push yourself to think from their perspective.

* If you mostly answered *A*, you understand the value of parent-teacher partnerships and are ready to get better at them.

Does This Get Any Easier?

Working with parents may not be easy, but it's worth the effort—and yes, it does get easier. When I was a young teacher working in a parent-cooperative nursery school, I called a mentor who had worked in another parent co-op for many years. I described the unreasonable expectations of the parents ("My child can sit still for an hour in church, I don't see why you aren't having her sit still and learn at school"), the lack of follow-through (parents forgetting to bring snack on their day or not staying to clean up after their day in the classroom), and their general lack of respect for my knowledge. My friend said to me, "It helps when you are old enough to be the parent's mother." "I'm not willing to wait that long!" I blurted out.

It didn't take that long. The more confident I got in my knowledge, the more the parents respected me. The more sure I was that my expectations of parents were reasonable, the more they followed through on those expectations. Most important, the more I relaxed and allowed myself to enjoy these people, the better my relationships with parents grew. I can now say that my work with parents has been one of the most enjoyable parts of my career in early childhood education.

This book was written to help bridge the difference in perspective between early childhood teachers and parents. You will see that your colleagues share the situations you find challenging. Each chapter will provide a framework for thinking through the different challenges to creating a family-friendly program. These factors include developing relationships with parents (chapter 1), program policies (chapter 2), program values (chapter 3), and issues about child development (chapter 4). Within each of these chapters, I have presented hypothetical problems so you can view the issue from multiple perspectives. This includes an explanation from the perspective of the teacher and the parent, ways to address the issue that creates a climate of partnership, what you can do (and not do) if this problem comes up, and ways to take problem solving a step further to truly create a family-friendly program.

Who am I to give you advice about working with parents? I am like you. I have taught in many kinds of programs, including Head Start, part-day nursery schools, and full-day programs. When I taught in a parent-cooperative program I was so frustrated trying to work with parents that I returned to graduate school to learn more about parent education and leadership. I eventually earned a master's degree from Pacific Oaks College with specialization in both early childhood education and parent/community work. I have since worked as a director and teacher in programs with many kinds of parents— parents of children with special needs, international parents, parents who are college students, and suburban parents. I have sought to have authentic working relationships with parents in all of these settings and to support teachers as they work with parents. I have taught courses including "Team Building for Parents and Teachers" and "Models and Methods of Parent Involvement," and I have found teachers who are eager to improve their relationships even if it can be scary.

I hope that the book provides some insight into how to improve your daily interactions with families.

Developing Relationships with Parents

The early childhood education field places a lot of stock in the importance of developing relationships between teachers and children. The "Relationships Among Teachers and Children" section of the National Association for the Education of Young Children (NAEYC) accreditation is heavily weighted in importance when programs are applying for accreditation. School entrance, orientation, style of interaction, scheduling—all are done with an eye on how relationships between children and teachers are built or hindered. If we believe that relationships between teachers and parents are critical to children's experiences, we must also work on developing these bonds as well.

Tips for Communicating with Parents

Remember those teachers we mentioned in the introduction? You know, the teachers that parents always want for their child? The ones to whom parents always want to talk, who can even give parents criticism and have parents listen to them. You can move toward being one of these teachers by building relationships through communication. You can take a number of steps to improve your communication with families:

1. Take time to develop lasting relationships with parents.
2. Be proactive with information.
3. Focus on the parents' perspective.
4. Talk it through with a colleague.
5. Take time to react.
6. Use the principles of active listening and respectful communication.
7. Give parents the benefit of the doubt.

Take Time to Develop Lasting Relationships with Parents

One mom describes her feelings for the teacher:

> *"My daughter loves her teacher, but that's not the only reason I am crazy about Terry. She's just a neat person! She really seems to care about me as well as Tiffany. She asks about my day, notices my mood, and shares funny stories about her own child. I feel so lucky to have Terry in our lives."*

It sounds simple, but it takes time and commitment. Think of the steps you take to build a relationship with a new child in your program. You approach her cautiously, giving her time to get used to your presence. You try to pick up cues from her and adjust your own behavior to be inviting without being overwhelming. You give her time to trust you. You demonstrate yourself to be likeable. You give her time to figure out that you are here to stay. You hope that you get a chance to have positive interactions with her before you have to set a limit or confront a negative situation.

The same is true of relationships with parents. Acknowledge that they are individuals just as their children are. Some are extroverts and will be easy to interact with. Others will take more time. Some will trust you instantly and others will need you to prove yourself. Treat your developing relationship with parents as deliberately and as individually as you do with children. Don't expect the same actions (a friendly greeting or small talk) to be received in the same way by all parents. Reflect on a budding relationship as you do with children and plan the next action with the understanding that a single formula won't work for all.

You know how to create relationships with children, but how do you go about it with adults? Here are six fundamental ways to lay the groundwork.

☀ **Be available.**
This doesn't mean chatting with parents when the children need your attention or staying after work for thirty minutes talking about a parent's new job. Instead, find a way to communicate with parents that

works for both of you. This may be a quick conversation at the beginning of the day, phone calls in the evening, or e-mail. If parents find you easy to talk to about little things, it will be easier for them to talk to you about difficult topics.

☀ Let parents lead the conversation.
Don't try to direct every conversation. Sometimes the parents who have something important to tell you need to get around to the topic in their own way.

☀ Be yourself.
Sometimes parents idealize their child's teacher. You seem to have all the answers. Their child doesn't misbehave with you as he does at home. A pedestal is a difficult place from which to build a relationship. Don't be afraid to show your faults. It is not useful for parents to think you are perfect.

☀ Share while staying within your own personal boundaries.
Teachers vary in their need for space from parents. This will not interfere in developing a relationship with parents. You do not need to be friends with the parents of the children you work with. It is also not inherently wrong to be friends with the parents in your class. There is no one right way.

Most parents respond positively to clear expectations from teachers. Some teachers are comfortable with more formal relationships—parents call them by their surnames and teachers keep personal information private. Other teachers may develop easy intimacy with families—they openly share information about their own families and lives outside of school. If the openness is sincere, many parents will respond. Parents may be more forthcoming with their own children's difficulties if they know the teacher has had similar battles.

☀ Be trustworthy.
What may seem like a small thing to you may feel like a betrayal of confidence to a parent. Always ask if information is public (for example, moving, making a major purchase, taking a new job, having a medical condition, or becoming engaged). If parents ask you for casual information about another parent, be clear and friendly in your refusal to give information. For example, if a parent asks you if another child's parent is pregnant, you can answer by saying, "I really can't talk about families, but you are welcome to ask her mom when she comes for pickup." While the parent may be momentarily embarrassed, they will remember that you were trustworthy.

☀ **Remember that the relationship is in service to the child, not your needs.**

Friendships with parents are tricky, especially during the time the child is in your care. Enter these relationships with caution. The child can easily get pushed out of the way while the adults are enjoying each other. Sometimes we need to tell parents hard truths, and our personal relationship with parents should not get in the way.

Be Proactive with Information

Emily's mom said the following:

> *"It was amazing! I drove up to pick up my child from school and there was an ambulance in the driveway. I ran up to the door, terrified that something had happened to Emily. There was the teacher, greeting us with information before we entered the classroom: 'The children are listening to a story with Sally (the other teacher). One of the children in our class had a seizure at school. We had to call an ambulance to care for her.' She then handed us a preprinted letter that addressed how to talk to our children about seizures, which they had written in case something like this happened. Because I was informed, I was able to calm Emily rather than having her deal with a scared mommy."*

Sometimes we avoid telling parents about less pleasant experiences in the hope that they won't find out and with the notion that what they don't know won't hurt them. The information may be for the whole parent body (a lice outbreak or a teacher leaving the program) or for a specific family (a child getting hurt at school or losing a belonging that is later found). This is a bad policy for two reasons. First, parents will not trust us if they learn teachers are keeping secrets. They will feel it is necessary to dig up information that is being hidden from them. As they investigate, we become less forthcoming and the relationship dissolves. Second, it is damaging for children to have experiences that their parents cannot help them understand. Even if parents never find out something you didn't want them to know, it is harder for children to deal with memories they are harboring if their parents do not know or understand their experience. Parents can accept almost anything if they are told honestly and assured mistakes won't happen again. I have known of parents forgiving teachers for forgetting children on field trips, accidentally hurting a child, saying something careless, and even losing control of their anger.

Share daily experiences with parents often enough that they are not startled by a request for communication. If parents are not accustomed to chatting with you or receiving written communication, contact will take on greater importance. Slipping something into conversation is easier when communication happens often. If you have information that is hard to share with a parent, keep the following in mind:

❋ **Keep a calm demeanor even if you are nervous.**

❋ **Don't forget to breathe!**
Parents pick up on nonverbal cues.

❋ **Begin with assurances that everything is okay.**
Sometimes people don't listen as they are waiting for the "punch line." A conversation about a child getting hurt can start: "She's okay now, but . . . ," or a conversation about a child's misbehavior can start: "She understands now, but . . ."

❋ **If you are unsure about the parent's reaction, don't bring it up in front of the child.**
If the child reacts to the tension between you and the parent, the whole situation can escalate.

❋ **Talk to the parent out of earshot of other parents.**
The worst thing that can happen is for another parent to hear part of the interaction. Because it would be inappropriate to tell the other parent about the communication due to issues of confidentiality, you would be unable to tell them anything about the conversation with the first parent. The parent who overheard can end up having to make up a story in her own mind to explain what was overheard. For example, a parent might overhear part of a conversation about a toy getting lost and assume that the teacher and parent were talking about a child getting lost.

❋ **Make arrangements for follow-up conversation if necessary.**
It might be that you have told the parent something they need to digest before the dialogue continues. Suggest the parent call you later or agree to meet him at school early the next day.

❋ **Avoid giving unwelcome news in writing before verbal contact.**
This is especially a problem with e-mail. If information needs to go in writing, it can follow a conversation. Don't forget that anything you put in writing can be read by others (including lawyers!), without the supporting context.

Focus on the Parent's Perspective

This parent believes her request is reasonable:

"I just asked if my daughter could stay awake during naptime. We are flying out tonight to visit my folks, and I wanted her to sleep on the plane. The teacher started telling me that she makes all her phone calls while the kids are sleeping and how it would be hard for her to keep my daughter awake. She's not the one who has to be on that plane with a restless child who won't sleep!"

If you start communication based on an understanding of the parents' perspective, you can choose your words more carefully. It is not the same as communicating with colleagues. Avoid using technical jargon. Terms such as *manipulatives*, *fine motor coordination*, and *self-regulation* may mean different things to parents. Give them information as it pertains to their child, their roles as parents, and how it affects their lives. They are less likely to be concerned with the needs of the whole class, your needs, or the school's needs than they are with their needs and the needs of their children. This is not a matter of being selfish. The parent's job is to think about the needs of her child and family. Your job is to balance the needs of all of the children and the program as a whole and to find a solution that works for everyone.

In order to keep yourself focused on understanding the parent's perspective so you can solve the problem, ask yourself questions like these:

❋ **How does this issue directly affect the parent?**
The impact on the class, the other children, the other families, or the teacher will not be viewed as the parent's problem.

❋ **What do you want the parent to do?**
It is fine to communicate "FYI" information to parents, but be clear that the information is your message. You are not asking for action. You may want to just let parents know that their child had a meltdown before lunch, but you don't expect them to do anything. If this meltdown is a continuing problem, you may ask the parents to take action. If you do want action, have a couple of alternatives in mind. Maybe you will suggest that the child eats breakfast or that the parents let you know if he doesn't eat so you can offer an earlier snack.

❋ **Are you keeping an open mind?**
If you are unwilling to accept any alternative solution, you are likely to experience conflict.

❋ **Are you truly listening to the parent's point of view?**
If you are thinking about how you are going to respond to what the parent is saying or prove her wrong, you are not truly listening.

Talk It Through with a Colleague

This teacher describes her problem:

> *"Boy, did I step in it. I just tried to mention to Mrs. Jones, as she was picking up Doug, that he pocketed a toy car today. Could she check to be sure he didn't have any other school toys at home. She just blew up! Said her child wasn't a thief! Made a scene in front of the other parents!"*

If you are a novice teacher, have particularly difficult information to share with a parent, or have not developed a positive relationship with the parent, you may benefit from practicing the conversation with a colleague. If the colleague will take the role of devil's advocate or even difficult parent, you can be better prepared for the conversation. Some questions to discuss together include the following:

❋ **What is the best timing for the topic?**
Sometimes it is important to talk to parents right away (before they hear about it from someone else, such as their child). At other times it is better to let everyone cool down before broaching the topic.

❋ **How will you bring up the topic?**
Talk through your opener. Should you be prepared with resources? If you are talking to a parent about a concern that involves his child, it will help if you can provide supporting articles, brochures, or community resource information.

❋ **Should you invite a colleague to join in the discussion?**
If tempers are likely to flare or you are concerned about being misquoted, having a coteacher or director with you might help. If nothing else, you might want to make sure someone else is in the building.

❋ **How can you share information as clearly as possible without being too blunt?**
You may find that role-playing the conversation with a coworker can help.

Take Time to React

Kiko is a new teacher:

> *"Timmy's mom asked me if I thought he was ready for kindergarten.
> I said, "Sure." I mentioned the conversation with the head teacher and
> she disagreed. She thinks he's too immature. I don't know how to
> bring it up to the mom now."*

If a parent brings an issue to you, don't be afraid to tell them you need to think about what they've said or gather more information. Here are some steps to keep you out of trouble:

1. **Take time to cool down if the conversation is heated or pushes your buttons.**
   You can't take back words once they are said.

2. **Make sure you have the authority to make promises if asked.**
   Giving permission to parents to do something out of the ordinary, and later telling them your supervisor doesn't approve, makes both you and your supervisor look bad.

3. **Take the time you need to gather information.**
   A school superintendent vowed to always return calls from parents within twenty-four hours, which sometimes proved to be a bad idea. She didn't take time to gather facts first. By taking the time to respond most appropriately, you demonstrate to parents that you are taking their issue seriously.

4. **If there is a delay in getting back to the parents, let them know you haven't forgotten.**
   If you are waiting for information, let them know what the holdup is (for example, you're waiting to speak to the director who is on vacation, or you want to check licensing regulations) and when you will respond. You don't want to give the impression you are ignoring the conversation in hopes the parents will forget about it.

Use the Principles of Active Listening and Respectful Communication

Rita shares how she uses experience from her personal life to improve her communication with parents:

> *"My husband and I are in counseling, and I find the same advice our
> counselor has for us about how to communicate also works well with*

the parents. I had a mom come to me, ready to really let me have it. She was mad because her daughter's stuffed animal was lost. I pulled her aside; listened to her without interrupting; and demonstrated that I understood her by saying, "This isn't the first time Boo-Boo has been lost. It's really frustrating, and I know Sierra can't sleep without Boo-Boo." Then I made a commitment for a short-term and a long-term solution: "Let's find Boo-Boo now, and tonight I'll think about how we can keep this from happening again." We looked around and found the bear, and the mom relaxed. She suggested buying another bear like Boo-Boo so it wouldn't be a problem if the bear was lost again. It was great that she went from being mad at me to feeling like we are a team."

Communication between parents and early childhood educators should reflect the best of what we know about respectful communication. We have ongoing relationships with parents, and strained communication won't help. Children notice the relationship between the important people in their lives—their parents and their teachers—and any tension between them will upset children. It is especially rewarding when you see the respectful communication techniques you are using find their way into the communication between parents and their children. Here are some cues for respectful communication:

❋ **Listen attentively.**
   Don't interrupt. Hear the feelings that drive the words.

❋ **Demonstrate that you understand the message of the parent.**
   Phrases such as "I hear you saying . . ." or "It sounds like . . ." may feel stilted when you try to use them, so find a way of expressing these ideas that fits you. Some teachers use "I wonder if . . ." or "Do you feel . . ." as other ways to reflect back.

❋ **Use words to express that you understand the issue from their perspective.**
   If parents don't think you get it, they may give up or become frustrated. When you show that you understand why they feel the way they do, parents will be ready to move to finding a solution. It also gives you the opportunity to correct your assumptions if you read the situation wrong. You might think a parent is angry when she is actually worried. If you don't understand, ask.

❋ **Be sure to avoid blaming the parent for the situation.**
   If you are raising a difficult issue, describe the problem in nonjudgmental terms, the consequences of the problem, and, if appropriate,

your feelings. It may be that your feelings need to be kept out of it to keep the interaction professional. For example, "When you are late picking up Abby, I am late picking up my daughter at her school, and she worries if I'm late."

✻ **Keep the conversation on track.**
If the parent becomes accusatory, don't take the bait. You can say, "I'm sorry you feel that way, but right now we need to find a solution for this issue that will work for all of us." If the parent brings up unrelated issues to put you on the defense, you can say, "Let's talk about that when we are done dealing with this issue." Be specific rather than general.

✻ **Avoid inflammatory words.**
Generalizing behavior makes people feel judged and defensive. Describe the events that need to be talked about (for example, "You have picked up Abby ten minutes late twice this week, and tonight you are thirty minutes late") rather than generalizing about the behavior (for example, "You are irresponsible about pickup time"). Words to avoid include *rude, disrespectful, selfish,* or other words you would not want people to use to describe you.

✻ **When you've found a solution, say it again to make sure you both heard the same thing.**
Restating is a way of clarifying and making sure that you have understood each other. Try saying something such as, "So you are going to write his name on his shoes. I will check after nap to see that they are in his cubby." The parent has a chance to hear the expectation and can correct it if necessary.

Give Parents the Benefit of the Doubt

Sharon shares what she learned:

> *"I used to get so annoyed with Felice's mother. I would give her information about school procedures. She'd nod and say, "Okay," but she would never follow through. I finally realized she doesn't understand English as well as I thought she did. Now I take more time to show her what I mean, and I can see in her eyes if she understands me."*

Lilian Katz believes that people tend to attribute their own mistakes to circumstances—traffic was bad, the clocks are wrong—and other people's mistakes to character flaws—she is flaky, she comes late because she likes to make an entrance (NAEYC Annual Conference, 1995, Washington, D.C., "The use of NAEYC's Code of Ethical Conduct within child care facilities").

The Dalai Lama says, "Assume positive intent." High expectations and a strong sense of forgiveness can go a long way in communication.

When Nothing Seems to Work

If you give up on working with a family, it may feel like a failure for you. Before you give up on establishing a relationship with a family, make sure there are good reasons beyond your own level of frustration. You may have reasons such as these:

☀ The relationship with the parent will only improve if you take steps that are unethical or illegal.

☀ The parent's lack of trust is having a negative impact on his child's school experience.

☀ The parent's lack of trust is having a negative impact on relationships with other families in the program.

☀ The parent makes staff members feel unsafe.

A parent who is uncomfortable with the ethnicity, gender, sexual preference, or age of a teacher needs to be educated on the benefits of diversity in the life of her child. By helping a parent work through this issue, you can have a profound effect on the child's life. Take time to help families work through knee-jerk responses to prejudices they might not have even been aware of. For instance, the benefits of having a positive male presence usually outweigh the possible negative fallout. You cannot break the law governing discriminatory hiring practices even if you know parents might be uncomfortable. Once parents develop trust, they will see the unique relationship their child can develop with a male caregiver. This is especially important for children who do not have many men in their lives.

If parents refuse to take part in working with their children's challenging behavior, the program administrator will have to decide if the child can be accommodated without change. This is a delicate balance of the needs of the individual child, other children in the program, and the staff. Here are some questions that may help you make a decision:

1. **Is the child disruptive?**

   If so, is he disruptive enough to make it difficult for the group to function? Are there changes that can be made to the program (the schedule, staffing, or expectations) that will alleviate the disruption?

2. **Is the child thriving in the program?**

   If not, are there changes that can be made (personal attention, new classroom) that will help the child to thrive and grow even if it is not as much as he might with professional intervention?

3. **Is the relationship with the family still sound enough to benefit the child?**

   Can parents and staff work together to meet the child's needs, or are too many bad feelings in the way? If it feels too hard, consider whether there is some way you can change your behavior or your feelings to make the situation better.

If a parent is spreading his negative attitude to other parents and is not responding to attempts from staff to improve the relationship, the family may need to be asked to leave the program.

Staff members need to feel physically and psychologically safe at work. I had a very volatile parent who accused her son's teacher of not liking her child as much as other children and told the teacher she would be "watching her like a hawk" for examples of her son not being treated fairly. I told the parent that we had to meet with the teacher to discuss her concerns before the child could return to school. When lack of trust turns to hostility, a teacher is at risk for accusations and will not feel safe in the workplace.

If you cannot establish a baseline of trust with a family that allows you to be effective with their child, you may have to help the family leave the program. Be candid with the family about your feelings to find out if the placement should continue. You might say, "We seem to be struggling to work together for your child. Perhaps you would be better served with a teacher with whom you can more easily build a rapport."

If it is not in the best interest of the child, family, or program to continue the child's enrollment, then make a transition plan with the family to minimize disruption for the child. Give the family ample opportunity to find another placement for their child, refer them to other programs, prepare the child and other children in the program for the change, and assist the family in enrollment in another program by providing records.

Scenarios

••

Scenario 1: What Is Going On at School?
or, Building Trust

One teacher complains:

"I have a parent who doesn't seem to believe anything I tell him. It's like he is trying to catch me in a lie. He asks about how his son's day went. When I share information, he looks skeptical and grills me for more information. The other day he asked if his son could come in on his day off. I explained that we have too many children on that day and we can't take another. I saw him going over the sign-in sheets and counting the children! Once his child came home with a cut on his elbow, and the dad asked me how he did it. I explained that he fell on the sidewalk. Not five minutes later, he was asking my teaching assistant what happened! How am I supposed to develop a relationship with a parent who doesn't trust me?"

Dad sees the problem differently:

"It's important to me that I am a responsible parent. My son is too young to always tell me what happens so I need to check to be sure everything is on the up-and-up. Sometimes, I think the school tries to take advantage of ignorant parents—making up rules to suit them. I am just making sure I understand the rules. The teacher is so defensive, it makes me wonder what she has to hide."

What Is the Problem?

Developing trust is often the first challenge to a relationship between a parent and teacher. Trusting others to care for your child can be scary. The younger the child, the more vulnerable she is, as the child cannot speak for herself. Expecting trust may seem reasonable—who would place their child in a program with people they don't trust? But trust comes in increments. The most basic trust, which needs to happen before a parent can leave their child in your care, is trust that their child will not be abused or stolen. Deeper levels of trust—caregivers will care about and for the child, like and perhaps love the child, understand the child enough to meet her needs; caregivers will interact with the child as they would at home and will not place the needs of other children before the needs of their child—develop more slowly. If a teacher or parent perceives a lack of trust, problems will arise in relationship building.

Once a climate of distrust has developed, you need to figure out if it can be repaired. Sit down with the family. You may want another person with you to help you communicate. Share what you have experienced with the family and your concern for how it may affect their child. Remember, it is not the family's job to care about you.

What Are You Thinking?

Be aware of how your reaction might make the situation worse. It is easier to move into finding positive solutions if you can avoid the following mind-sets, recognizing them as unhelpful to developing a healthy partnership with parents. Typical defensive reactions include the following:

※ *"The parent doesn't think I am trustworthy."*
It is hard to keep from personalizing suspicions from parents. Rather, give parents the benefit of the doubt and stay as open as possible. Defensiveness can confirm the parent's feeling of suspicion.

※ *"The parents will undermine my relationship with the child."*
Children are likely to pick up safety cues from parents. Telling parents to stop acting distrustful in front of their children is not likely to help. Children pick up on the feelings of their parents. When their words, feelings, and actions do not match, it will confuse the child.

※ *"The parents will ruin my reputation with other parents."*
You cannot control relationships between parents. Parents will share concerns with other parents, and all you can do is hope that your relationship with most parents is strong enough for them to ignore the concerns of others.

※ *"This parent is looking for an excuse to remove her child from my school (or class or home)."*
Sometimes parents need a face-saving reason for removing a child from a program when embarrassing factors require a change. It is much easier to tell friends that the program or teacher wasn't good enough than it is to say you can't afford the program or you need longer hours than the program provides. You can make it easier for a parent to remove their child from the program by being gracious about the exit, so they don't need to find evidence against you.

What Are Parents Thinking?

Thinking about how our actions strike emotional chords with parents (just as theirs do with us) can help us to be more sensitive.

☀ *"Here we go again."*
Parents who have experienced a profound lack of fairness in their own lives, especially families who are not from the dominant culture, are often eager to protect their children from that experience. If parents are suspicious of you, they may have been lied to in similar situations in the past. It is important to give the message that your treatment of all families will be fair. This is not about you, it's about society. For some families, you will need to be overt about fairness rather than thinking it will be assumed. Tell families how you have ensured fairness when an action or policy implies fairness (such as enrollment or placement in programs, variable tuition rates, or discipline policies).

☀ *"This teacher only shares information with my wife, as if she's the real parent and I am not."*
Trust can be difficult for both dads and moms for different reasons. Most men are going to feel in the minority in a preschool environment, and most are unaccustomed to that feeling. Separated parents may be especially sensitive. Noncustodial parents can feel out of the loop or that the school takes the side of the custodial parent (often the mother). Mothers can feel powerless to advocate for themselves or their children. If you think a parent is having a difficult time expressing her needs or those of her children, take the time to clarify.

Solving the Problem

Each situation will require unique solutions, but the following are some paths you might take.

☀ *Ask the parent if they are getting the information they need from you.*
Say something such as, "I am wondering if I am keeping you informed enough about class events. Is a short talk at pickup time working for you?"

☀ *Listen to the parents' comments without defensiveness.*
If you allow them to talk without being interrupted, they may get past negative feelings and figure out what they really want. They may realize you are not the person they are struggling with. They may share things you have said or nonverbal communication messages they have picked up from you that you are unaware of. When your eyes dart from the parent to a child, the parent may read that move as disinterest rather than you being hypervigilantly keeping an eye on the class.

☀ *Share your desire for communication.*
Say something such as, "I wish I had time to talk to you at pick-up time as well. It seems like as soon as you walk in the door, something comes up that takes my attention."

☀ *Ask for suggestions.*
See what the parent thinks would help to improve information sharing, and create a plan that everyone can live with. "Would phone calls or notes work better?"

After the Problem Is Solved: Moving Toward True Partnership

Building trust takes time and if you stick with the family during the process, it can be very rewarding. Some of the families that teachers struggled with the most eventually established such a strong foundation of trust, they continued to seek our counsel when their child entered high school. The other benefit is that often families have several children go through the program. You can enjoy a foundation of trust from the beginning with the siblings.

Offer families regular opportunities to fill out anonymous questionnaires, giving feedback, assessing the program, and reviewing your performance. Being able to put their concerns on the table might help them let go. It also gives you feedback from many satisfied families.

Before You Have a Problem

Read through the following list and check off what you have already accomplished (see pages 2–12). If many of the checkboxes are blank, you have work to do to solve the problem and create an environment where problems are easy to solve.

☐ *Begin by building a relationship.*
Acknowledge the need to build trust. When you first meet the family, acknowledge that trust takes time. This can help parents relax and understand that their feelings are natural. If they think they shouldn't feel that way, they may be looking for an explanation of what triggered their reaction.

☐ *Be proactive with information.*
Share information without fail. Even if you aren't sure that parents need to know something, tell them anyway. Tell them about the scratch on their child's knee, the tears the child cried at rest time, the lunch box you lost. Do so matter-of-factly—you are presenting information that parents need to have. Your honesty will build trust.

☐ *Focus on the parents' perspective.*
Use the principles of active listening and respectful communication. Listen to parents' concerns without defensiveness. Try to be reassuring without being condescending. Remember that teaching parents to trust others is your job as much as teaching children to trust others.

● ●

Scenario 2: Fear of Men, Strangers, and Dangerous Persons, or, The Boogeyman

One teacher shares her dilemma:

"We had our parent open house at the beginning of the year. Mrs. Johnson asked me about the student interns, so I told her about Joe. She became pale. "A man? I don't feel comfortable with that. Maybe I can get my daughter switched into the other class."

Mrs. Johnson explains:

"You read so much about child molesters. I know that they are usually men. It seems like pedophiles get jobs where they have access to children. I would never forgive myself if something happened to my daughter. It just doesn't seem worth taking the chance."

What Is the Problem?

Emotionally, leaving your child with others is risky enough. Asking parents to accept placing their children in the care of someone they find suspect is even tougher.

Consciousness is heightened in new situations. Just as you begin noticing red Volkswagens once you buy one, placing their child in care makes parents notice any new article about children in child care. Parents read about molestation stories. They know that they are ultimately responsible for what happens to their children. They may be receiving comments and even pressure from relatives. A generation ago it was less common for men to be involved in the care of children and to some people, it seems unnatural.

What Are You Thinking?

Be aware of how your reaction might make the situation worse. It is easier to move into finding positive solutions if you can avoid getting into the following mind-sets, recognizing them as unhelpful to developing a healthy partnership with parents. Typical defensive reactions include the following:

☀ *"The parent doesn't trust my judgment."*
   We like to believe that the families we work with trust our decisions unconditionally, but it's appropriate for parents to scrutinize decisions that affect their children. That's their job!

☀ *"Parents are interfering with staffing decisions."*
   Parents want and need to know who is caring for their children. You would not approve if parents left their children with a babysitter they

didn't know. They also need to know who is taking care of their children in provider-based care.

❄ *"The parent is going to make unfair accusations."*
Unfounded charges of abuse have been a major concern of caregivers for over a decade. The best way to avoid accusations is to keep the parents as informed and involved as possible. If parents feel free to take advantage of an open-door policy, they learn they have nothing to fear.

What Are Parents Thinking?

Thinking about how our actions strike emotional chords with parents (just as theirs do with us) can help us to be more sensitive.

❄ *"Why would a man want to work with young children?"*
Some people are less comfortable with men caring for children than others. Is the concerned parent ethnically different from you? Is she a single mother who may have less experience leaving her child in the care of a male? Is there a religious issue? Knowing the answers to these questions will not necessarily change your policies, but may give you insight into how to best approach the family.

Solving the Problem

If a parent has questioned the appropriateness of a staff member, you may find it hard to keep from becoming defensive. You can help by providing reassurances.

❄ *Explain why you have selected this person to join your staff.*
Share what you like about him, special qualifications he has (including his personality), and the extent of your reference check.

❄ *Share the benefits of having men as caregivers.*
It will not have occurred to some parents that nurturing men can enrich their children's lives.

❄ *Share positive stories from your experiences.*
It can help to share specific stories about how educators who are men have had a positive impact on the lives of children.

❄ *Explain the precautions you will take to protect all children and staff.*
It is especially important to protect the men on staff from suspicion. Will he (or any other staff member) be alone with children when toileting or dressing? These activities place men at risk for accusations and may not be worthwhile. If he is teaching alone, will people drop into the classroom unannounced? This may give parents confidence.

After the Problem Is Solved:
Moving Toward True Partnership

Can you include parent representatives in the hiring process? When parents have personal investment in a staff member's success, they share their enthusiasm with other families.

Before You Have a Problem

Read through the following list and check off what you have already accomplished (see pages 2–12). If many of the checkboxes are blank, you have work to do to solve the problem and create an environment where problems are easy to solve.

☐ *Begin by building a relationship.*
Introduce parents to all staff. Provide introductions in person or through written notices. Have photos and short biographies posted or in promotional materials. Include background information about each staff member. Knowing that he is someone's son, father, uncle, friend, and so on makes him seem safer. The best way to avoid demonizing a person is by getting to know him or her.

☐ *Be proactive with information.*
Write policy statements and share your safety precautions. The parent handbook can prepare parents for inclusion of men on the staff. Most parents aren't aware of required or voluntary background checks on staff members. Sharing that you have researched possible criminal records relieves parents. Start the process of parents and staff meeting each other sooner. If parents aren't caught by surprise, they are less likely to react.

· ·

Scenario 3: The Parent Who Drains You, or, "Excuse me, but I have some children here who need my attention."

This teacher is overwhelmed by the needs of parents:

"Sarah's mom is so needy. She is single and has no family in this area. I know she's had some health problems as well. But she acts like our job is to take care of her instead of taking care of Sarah. She comes in when we are in the middle of group time and she always has ten things she has to tell us, like who is picking up Sarah, phone numbers for where we can reach her, some new worry she has from reading her magazines. It's the same routine when she picks up. My teaching partner and I both just want to hide when she comes. She volunteers to help in the classroom on Wednesdays but then she wants to spend the whole time talking to me instead of working with the children. No offense, but I don't need another girlfriend!"

Sarah's mom explains:

"It is so hard taking care of Sarah by myself. Her father is such a flake—he makes all kinds of promises but he always lets us down. Sarah is my whole life. I spend a lot of time at her school so I can be the best mother possible. But sometimes it seems like the teachers just don't want to know about Sarah's time at home. They don't seem very friendly when I come into the classroom. It makes me wonder if everything is okay. I mean, don't they want parents to be involved?"

What Is the Problem?

If a parent has already established a habit of demanding your attention, you need to gently wean her off it. If you withdraw too suddenly, the parent may think she has done something wrong and put more energy into reconciling. It can be helpful to find a replacement: "Talk to Betsy's mom about that—she mentioned that too."

What Are You Thinking?

Be aware of how your reaction might make the situation worse. It is easier to move into finding positive solutions if you can avoid getting into the following mind-sets, recognizing them as unhelpful to developing a healthy partnership with parents. Typical defensive reactions include these:

☀ ***"This parent is taking over my classroom."***
Parents don't always realize that we keep a constant vigil on our classrooms. It appears that we spend some time just standing around. Parents don't think that they are distracting us from observing the children.

☀ ***"This parent expects me to socialize with her and it interferes with my private life."***
As difficult as it may be, it's kinder to refuse invitations for social time, if you don't want to attend.

What Are Parents Thinking?

Thinking about how our actions strike emotional chords with parents (just as theirs do with us) can help us to be more sensitive.

☀ ***"She loves my daughter so much, we have a strong connection. We could be friends."***
Some parents are more isolated and so are needier than others. This can be true of parents who have moved from a different country or single parents. While you should not socialize more than you are comfortable doing, you also shouldn't worry that you need to have the same relationship with all parents.

Solving the Problem

☀ *Acknowledge the parent's need for contact.*
Say something such as, "I can tell you really appreciate the time you spend in our classroom."

☀ *Let the parent know that the children are your first priority.*
Say something such as, "I'm sorry that at times it seems like I am ignoring you, but the children need my constant attention."

☀ *Suggest other modes of communication.*
Say something such as, "Since I can't stop to give you directions when you come in to do a project with the children, how about if I leave written instructions for you on the clipboard?"

☀ *Avoid sending double messages.*
If you say, "Maybe we can meet for coffee sometime," and then you avoid making a firm date, the parent is left confused. Instead, you can say, "When I am not at work my family (or studies or personal life) requires all of my energy. I'm sorry I won't have time for social engagements with school families."

❋ *Try to help the parent connect with others.*
You can suggest that she join a parenting club if there is one in your area or mention a fellow parent that lives in the area she might be able to socialize with.

After the Problem Is Solved: Moving Toward True Partnership

Why not include social support for parents as part of your job? If you know that a parent is especially needy, arrange with your coworkers to cover for you so you have time to chat with the parent. It may be a greater service for the child than you can perform in the classroom.

Before You Have a Problem

Read through the following list and check off what you have already accomplished (see pages 2–12). If many of the checkboxes are blank, you have work to do to solve problems and create an environment where problems are easy to solve.

☐ *Begin by building a relationship.*
Set clear limits from the beginning. For some parents, teachers are their only constant contact with adults. They develop trust in us and appreciate that we love their children. Sometimes, they infringe upon our boundaries and want us to become a part of their social circle. We may be the only people who give them attention and they come to depend on it. It is tricky to establish limits without hurting their feelings. Set limits from the beginning. It is easier to set boundaries to begin with and is less likely to leave a parent feeling deserted.

☐ *Be proactive with information.*
Set boundaries. If a parent wants your attention when you need to be with the children, let him know that this isn't a good time but he can call (or e-mail) you later.

☐ *Focus on the parents' perspective.*
Help isolated parents connect with other parents. Offer social events for families and steer parents toward conversation with each other. Caring for parents' social needs is a natural part of a family-friendly program. A volunteer parent can arrange family social events. Some schools have group camping trips, family outings on weekends, and other activities to support parents.

☐ *Use the principles of active listening and respectful communication.*
Give nonverbal messages that now is not the time to chat. If you are on
the floor when the parent enters, stay there rather than rising to talk. The
parent is then forced to bend down or join you on the floor, which usually keeps conversations short. Demonstrate the need for you to break
away from social conversation by leaving suddenly to deal with a child.
Keep your eyes on the children rather than on the parent to send a clear
message about your priorities.

Scenario 4: Recommending a Child for Assessment, or, "What is wrong with Tim?"

One teacher shares:

"I have been working with children for years, and I have good instincts about when something is just a phase a child is going through and when there is a problem. We've been talking to Tim's parents since he started the year. We gave him the benefit of the doubt for the first month of school, but he just wasn't catching on to routines as fast as I expected. We let his parents know what was going on. We'd give them a quick report at pick-up time, and they seemed like they appreciated the information. We had our first parent-teacher conferences this week where we told his parents we wanted to have Tim screened. We had the papers right there and everything so we could get right on it. The educational coordinator of our program was there too so she could explain how the process worked. Tim's parents seemed really eager to follow through and signed the papers right away. They asked if we thought they should take him to a child psychologist, and we advised them to wait until we saw the screening results. Well, that was Friday, and they haven't brought Tim to school all week. Wednesday they called the director, really upset, ready to take Tim out of the school. They told her that we don't like Tim! What happened between Friday and Monday?"

Tim's parents explain:

"We put Tim in a new school this year, and we've been really happy until now. The teachers really seemed on top of things. We had confidence that all was well. On Friday we had our first conference and found out that the teachers think something is really wrong with Tim. We had no warning and just walked into this meeting to find one of the program administrators there with papers to sign to have Tim tested for being autistic or something. We were so shocked, we didn't know what to say. I felt so ashamed that my son was in such trouble and I didn't even know it! They seemed to have it all together—knew who we could take our child to—so we were relieved that there was a plan of action. Once we got home I called my sister-in-law who is a psychologist. She said there's nothing wrong with Tim. The behavior the teachers described is perfectly normal, she says. We were relieved that she didn't think there was anything wrong with Tim but now we realize that the teachers think he is a problem. We don't feel like we should even bring him back there."

What Is the Problem?

Multiple issues are involved in this case. Most are related to the teachers and parents not understanding each other's perspective. One of parents' greatest fears is that there is something wrong with their child.

☀ *Parents are worried about their children's future.*
One of the important phases in a parent's development is the imagining phase (Galinsky 1980), when they make pictures in their minds of their children as adults, including their occupations and families. A possible developmental delay can change that image.

☀ *Parents may feel guilty.*
It's hard to think that someone else noticed something about their child that they missed. If parents can't trust doctors and other professionals, what else could they have missed?

☀ *Parents may blame themselves.*
It's easy for parents to feel responsible if something is wrong with their child. Was it their genes? They may remember relatives that have had problems. Was it bad parenting? Maybe it's from that glass of wine mom had when she was pregnant or from going back to work too soon or being too permissive.

What Are You Thinking?

Be aware of how your reaction might make the situation worse. It is easier to move into finding positive solutions if you can avoid getting into the following mind-sets, recognizing them as unhelpful to developing a healthy partnership with parents. Typical defensive reactions include these:

☀ *"If I don't get this child help, I will be irresponsible."*
You are aware of the benefits of early intervention. In the past few years, teachers have felt a greater sense of alarm over early identification. The bottom line: it is ultimately the parents' responsibility.

☀ *"These parents are just in denial."*
It is hard to be patient while parents work through their own feelings. It is hard for a teacher who has not been a parent to relate to the complexity of emotions a parent who is confronted with this possibility might feel.

☀ *"They don't trust my judgment."*
When confronted with something you don't want to believe, it is natural to look to others to support your position. If teachers are not gracious about parents' need to get corroboration, they may permanently damage the relationship they have with them.

What Are Parents Thinking?

Thinking about how our actions strike emotional chords with parents (just as theirs do with us) can help us to be more sensitive.

❋ *"The teacher doesn't understand my child."*
Behaviors that may seem atypical in a child may be more typical of children in her cultural group. Self-help skills (feeding, dressing, toileting) are expected at an early age by mainstream American culture. But in some cultures, these skills are not expected or taught until much later. Second-language learners may understand less than they appear to. Keep in mind that a child's atypical behavior may be related to how much they understand what you've told her.

❋ *"The teacher is saying my child is dumb!"*
Different cultural groups have varied attitudes toward doctors, mental health specialists, and differently abled people. Do your homework to find out about families' attitudes and beliefs before talking to them about concerns.

Solving the Problem

If you plan to talk to parents about concerns about their child's development, you can take steps to ensure a positive outcome. When approached with sensitivity, parents can team with teachers to learn about a child's needs and how to best meet them.

❋ *Provide parents information about screening.*
Learn whether the health insurance carried by the parents provides screening, or pass on the names of public organizations that can provide evaluation. If parents are resistant to recommendations that their child be assessed, you will need to ensure that you have given parents clear information, make resources available, and repair any uneasiness between family and school.

❋ *Take a step back.*
Assure parents that you have their child's best interests at heart, and give them time to think through your suggestions. Be clear in your attitude and in your behavior. The parents are the decision-makers where their child is concerned.

❋ *Be conscious of your behavior toward both the child and family.*
The parents may be a little wary or defensive as a result of the interaction. Be sure that you do not react defensively or cautiously. The family needs to know that nothing has changed.

☀ *Make a plan with the parents to meet again.*
Give parents time to think about what you have said, and then plan to
discuss the issue again. Arrange it for a time that works for them and invite them to bring along a support person, such as a grandparent or
family friend.

☀ *Cooperate in screening.*
Many screening tools include checklists or questionnaires to be com-
pleted by the teacher.

☀ *Be available for parents' questions or concerns during the process.*
Parents have a lot of information to absorb and decisions to make. You
can help.

☀ *Learn what you can about meeting the needs of this child.*
Identifying a child as having special needs doesn't make that child a
lesser member of your class. Often, special educators, speech pathologists, and other therapists recommend to do just the kinds of activities
that we typically provide in preschool. Rather than focusing on a diagno-
sis, find out what you can do to help a child with this specific set of behaviors or gaps in understanding. Share your successes with parents.

After the Problem Is Solved: Moving Toward True Partnership

Teachers can be great assets to a team putting together an Individual
Educational Plan (IEP) for a child with a disability or delay. Home visits from
the teaching staff can add insight, as can encouraging parents to observe
the child in school. If the child needs special services, a teacher can be an
important member of the team even if services are provided elsewhere.
Ideas for classroom routines and activities can be suggested by speech
pathologists, occupational therapists, and other specialists. Teachers can
offer ideas for favorite activities and ways for winning the child's cooperation
with the specialists. It is a great relief for parents to have the teacher they
have learned to trust involved in their child's special education.

Before You Have a Problem

Read through the following list and check off what you have already accomplished (see pages 2–12). If many of the checkboxes are blank, you have
work to do to solve problems and create an environment where problems
are easy to solve.

☐ *Begin by building a relationship.*
Share information with parents over time. Have at least three conversa-tions with parents to report positive comments about their child before talking to them about something difficult. It is important for parents to know you like their child and see his positive qualities before addressing concerns. Yes, early intervention is important but a few months are not going to be as detrimental for the child as it is for parents whose own feelings are out of control.

☐ *Be proactive with information.*
Invite parents to spend time in the classroom. If parents see how their child behaves when compared to other children in her class, they may al-ready have a feeling for what you tell them.

☐ *Focus on the parents' perspective.*
Find out how parents view their child. This can happen in a conference before the child enters the program or, ideally, in a home visit. Communicate with parents with an open mind. Listen to what they have to say about their child and give their opinions credence. There may be other explanations for the behavior you see.

☐ *Take time to react.*
Record observations of the child so you have clear examples to give par-ents. Share your observations and thoughts.

Discussion Questions

1. What kind of relationship did your parents have with the programs you attended as a child? How do you think that affected you as a child? What might have strengthened your parents' relationship with your school?

2. Make a list of the parents you get along with the most easily. What do they have in common? Make a list of the parents you have more troubling relationships with. See if you can find similarities that do not blame or judge these families. What steps can you take to move more families from list two to list one?

3. What steps do you take to make parents feel comfortable in your classroom? What else can you try?

☀ 2 ☀

Policies That Work
for Families and Staff

Written policies have a strong effect on families' experiences in a program. A clearly written policy gives parents the power of information and can help them to feel less vulnerable to the whims of a teacher or administrator. It can give a teacher the leverage to insist on actions that reflect the program's philosophy. It can ensure consistency from one similar situation to the next.

How policies are set and carried out often demonstrates attitudes about children, families, and staff. Policies can reflect defensive positions that assume families and program staff are adversaries or permissive positions that place the wishes of the few over the needs of others, or they can be carefully thought-out and applied, and designed to serve the range of needs of all the parties involved.

Some attitudes drive policies that do not reflect a climate of partnership.

1. The Lead Foot—when policies start with the assumption that if you give an inch, parents will take a mile. "If we let her do that, we'll have to let everyone." This reflects a lack of understanding that people and situations vary. When parents experience rules without reason, their reaction is typical to all humans—fighting against tyranny by breaking the rules.

2. The Oil Can—the habit of oiling the "squeaky wheel," the parent who complains. The rules are ignored with a whisper of "Don't tell anyone

else I am letting you do this." The message is that either the rule wasn't valuable enough to enforce or that all rules are up for grabs. If you aren't ashamed of your actions, why keep them a secret? Rather than garnering loyalty from parents, it encourages them to push harder to get their way. It also places less assertive parents at a disadvantage.

3. The Door Mat—giving in to all demands in a philosophy of "the customer is always right." Early childhood educators tend to be uncomfortable with conflict and sometimes will do anything to avoid it. When administrators take this approach, they place staff in a difficult place of having to advocate for themselves and rob parents of hearing the teacher's perspective on how policies affect their children.

So what is the alternative? Developing policies based on the values and goals of the families and staff of the program. If a policy can be drawn back to the program philosophy and goals, it is no longer about power struggles. It's about how the community of the program can best meet the needs of all the members.

Principles of Setting and Following Family-Friendly Policies

Three steps will give you a context for thinking about how to set and carry out policies:

1. Create fair policies that support the mission and goals of the program.
2. Tell parents about policies before enrollment.
3. Develop and tend to your relationships with parents.

Step One: Create Fair Policies

The first step is creating fair policies that support the mission and goals of the program. To do this you need to make policies that are consistent with rules that affect your program; write down the policies and distribute them; write the policies as clearly as you can; and be clear about consequences for not following them.

Know the laws and rules that affect your program and create policies that are consistent with these rules. For example, most programs are governed by some form of licensing. Rules about health and safety are affected by licensing standards. The National Association for the Education of Young Children (NAEYC) has a voluntary accreditation system. Setting policies that are in conflict with NAEYC's criteria limits the ability to become an accredited program. Most programs are responsible for adhering to the Americans with Disabilities Act (ADA). Creating policies that exclude children and staff with special needs are likely to be in conflict with this law.

Write down your policies, and make sure all staff and parents have copies. Many preschool programs enjoy a level of informality that seems inconsistent with written policies. Remember, when the policy is written, employees and parents who join the community have the opportunity to know what they are signing on for.

Write policies clearly. Avoid jargon or legalese. If parents don't understand what you are saying, you can't expect them to comply. State clearly if there are exceptions made (for example, rules about enrolling only toilet-trained children may exempt children with special needs, or different rules may exist for different ages of children).

Be up front with the consequences of not following policies. It may seem negative to bring up consequences in the beginning. But people deserve to know what could happen, and it takes the pressure off you if you must follow through. Avoid giving double messages. We tend to want to be nice and say, "That's okay," when it clearly is not.

Step Two: Tell Parents about Policies before Enrollment

The second step is to inform parents about policies before they enroll their child. Merely handing out a parent handbook and expecting parents to read and understand the ramifications of all policies is unreasonable. A parent who visits multiple programs to make a placement is overwhelmed with information. Be sensitive to the culture and first language of parents, which can affect both the parents' understanding of policies and their comfort in bringing up concerns.

Spend time talking about policies when parents tour the school. For example, if you have strict hours of operation, make that clear. Some programs allow parents to sign up for extra hours as needed and they may assume you do the same.

Talk to parents as their children are enrolling. Make it safe for parents to share conflicts and concerns about policies. If they sense that you might not accept their child into the program if they question policies, they may not verbalize their feelings. It is better to work through any compromises or special circumstances before the child begins.

Give reasons for policies. Some parents really bristle at hearing "That's the policy" and need a good reason to follow it, especially if it makes their lives more difficult.

For example, it might not be obvious to parents that if your program is *campus-related,* it means that your calendar is linked to the schedule of the college.

Step Three: Develop and Tend to Your Relationships with Parents

The third step is to develop and tend to your relationships with parents. It is important to develop rapport and a sense of trust with families before conflicts come up. If you have established a good, trusting relationship with parents, it will be easier to get them to comply with policies they don't agree with, especially when they understand that it is important to you.

Be flexible and compromise whenever possible. Keep your eye on the reason for the policy rather than the policy itself. Rules have a way of taking on a life of their own! It's easy to shift focus from supporting the mission and goals of the program to making people comply with the rules without thinking about why the rules exist. Work with the parents to figure out what the child's need is, and try to find a way to address it.

Avoid making judgments about parents' concerns or disagreements with policies. To imply that you know what is better for a child than the parents is likely to offend them. Explain the difference between what is successful at home and what works well in your program setting. You may have strong feelings about toy weapons and young children, but families who hunt or work for the Department of Defense may have different values. It will be less offensive to these parents if you say, "We find classroom management easier if we don't allow toy weapons," rather than, "We believe that playing with toy weapons is bad for children and encourages aggression."

Understand that parents' first concerns are for their child's happiness. It is unreasonable to expect parents to place as much importance on what makes the class run more smoothly or what is fair for the other children as they do on their own child's experience. Help parents see how a policy makes a better, happier learning experience for their child.

Ask for parents' help in developing policies that will work for teachers and families. This can be done formally or informally. I have always had an advisory committee of parents and community members to run policies by and to help invent them. Not only do they come up with great ideas, but it is easier for parents to buy into rules when they have a voice. When parents wanted to change a policy, this group provided a forum for them to be heard. Here is an example: a parent wanted us to change our policy of allowing only adults to sign out children from the center. This parent wanted her thirteen-year-old daughter to get off the school bus at our center and walk her younger daughter home. I was not comfortable with allowing this exception to the policy and suggested the parent make her case to the committee. Committee members asked questions including these: What if there is a lightning storm—who would get your children home then? What if your children were followed home by a stranger? In the end, the committee did not recommend rescinding the policy, but the parent left feeling that her request had been given serious consideration.

Ask parents for feedback on policies and take their answers into consideration for revision. I have a questionnaire that goes out to all parents each year, and I have an exit survey. Parents are given a chance to reflect on their experiences, and we learn from their experience at the center.

When Nothing Seems to Work

What should you do if families refuse to follow policies? Generally, teachers are quick to want families tossed out of schools when they are caught in power struggles. By nature we tend to be people who don't enjoy conflict—that's why we didn't go to law school! At times conflict is so uncomfortable that we want to move quickly to sever the relationship. Honestly, the best experience I ever had working with parents was in a program where it wasn't an option to make families leave because the program was publicly funded. We all knew we had to work things out, and it made us very creative problem-solvers! In many ways it was a relief to have the possibility of asking the family to leave taken off the table.

Asking families to leave should always be a last resort. Here are some guidelines for taking action when you have come to a stalemate.

1. **Decide if the issue is important enough to lose a child in your program.**

   Once you have locked in a power struggle, parents may withdraw their child from the program. Situations that may warrant severe reactions include these:

   ❀ The safety of children is involved. If not following school policy places children in danger, you may be unable to avoid conflict.

   ❀ There are legal consequences for you. If parents are ignoring policies that are mandated (signing in and out, for instance), you cannot place yourself and your program in jeopardy.

   ❀ The lack of parental compliance escalates. Sometimes people have issues with authority and rules. If parents are unable to accept that you need to set some parameters, the power struggle may never end. You can put your foot down now, or put your foot down later.

❀ The lack of compliance has a negative effect on other families. In most programs, families are aware of what the others do and say. If you are making an exception to rules that you cannot justify to yourself, what will you say to other parents when they ask? You may need to take a stand to keep resentment from growing among the other families.

2. If you want to keep the family in the program, you can try the following:

❀ Ask the parent for help in finding a solution. If they realize how critical this issue is for you, they may have an idea you didn't think of.

❀ Share the issue (confidentially) with other professionals. Chat rooms, such as NAEYC's Members Only Web site, are wonderful resources. You can get ideas from asking participating teachers how they have handled such issues.

❀ Examine the match between your own values and those of the school. Sometimes, it is the teacher who is not on the same page as the rest of the school community. If a policy is much more important to you than it is to others, you may be in the wrong school.

Scenarios

. . . .

Scenario 1: Parents Who Don't Follow School Rules, or, "But we're special!"

You can hear Sally's frustration:

"We have a clearly stated policy: No toys from home. It's in our parent handbook. When kids bring toys from home, parents blame us if they are lost or broken. Kids end up fighting over toys all the time, which takes away from the activities we set up for them. Tasha keeps bringing these stupid McDonald's toys. All the kids get excited, and she controls the whole class while she decides who gets to hold it. Someone ends up in tears and I have to take the toy away. I have brought this up to her mother repeatedly. I am ready to frisk her when she enters school."

Tasha's mom is also frustrated:

"I don't know why the teacher has to be so uptight about toys from home. It is so hard to get my daughter to leave for school in the morning, and taking a toy with her makes it so much easier. I don't care if it is lost or broken. Tasha says she understands that she is taking a risk, and I don't let her bring anything important anyway. It just makes things so much easier for us. I think the school could be flexible about this. They want flexibility from us, don't they?"

What Is the Problem?

The main issue here for the teacher is usually control over the classroom environment and emotional climate. The teacher wants to choose what equipment is available for children. The parent does not see it this way—home toys and school toys are just toys. She wants her child to be happy to go to school.

Sometimes, parents may want to change the program and learning environment you have created. If they send workbooks, phonics videos, and other teaching tools, it may be a signal that they do not understand (or accept) your educational philosophy.

What Are You Thinking?

Be aware of how your reaction might make the situation worse. It is easier to move into finding positive solutions if you can avoid getting into the following mind-sets, recognizing them as unhelpful to developing a healthy partnership with parents. Typical defensive reactions include these:

☀ *"The parent doesn't respect my authority."*
You may think the parents are purposely defying school policy, while the parents may think that the policy is a suggestion rather than a rule.

☀ *"Toys from home encourage commercialism and competition between children."*
Remember that parents are not likely to observe the subtle changes that occur in your classroom in reaction to toys.

☀ *"Toys from home take the focus away from my curriculum."*
It is frustrating to have worked hard developing plans for classroom activities that are then usurped for other activities that you see as having little value. Remember, parents experience the dynamic interest of their children rather than focusing on one interest or topic at a time. They aren't going to be as invested in your daily or weekly curriculum plan.

☀ *"Other educators and parents will think badly of me if I have Barbies (or weapons, Disney toys, or coloring books) in my classroom."*
You are proud of the environment you create and want to be judged by what you intend rather than by what others bring into the environment. This is especially challenging in high-visibility sites such as lab schools. Try to keep your ego out of the equation. Remember that being flexible to meet the needs of families and children is just as much of a philosophical rock to stand on as Developmentally Appropriate Practice is.

What Are Parents Thinking?

Thinking about how our actions strike emotional chords with parents (just as theirs do with us) can help us to be more sensitive.

☀ *"The teacher thinks I'm a bad parent for letting my daughter have this toy."*
It can feel judgmental to parents if they get the impression you think they provide their children with inappropriate toys. Toy choices are values choices. Toy guns, toy make-up, fashion-model dolls, and flash cards reflect values. It is critical to be sensitive. For example, toy weapons can be as much a part of life as other pretend items.

☀ *"I saved for a long time to give my child this toy, and the teacher doesn't even care."*
Parents with limited resources may be very proud of a fancy doll or other expensive toy their child has. Your lack of acceptance of it in the classroom may feel hurtful.

☀ *"The teachers have to say, "No toys," but I don't think it's that important to them as long as I don't fuss if it gets lost."*
Some cultures base their communication on negotiation more than others do. Some families may think that a rule is a starting place, and practice depends on personal negotiations. What seems like good bargaining to them may feel like a challenge to you.

☀ *"The teacher wants my child to be just like her kids."*
Trust can also be an issue if there is a difference between the cultural values of the family and your own values. Parents may correctly assume that you do not share their values for their children (such as expectations for compliance, problem solving, or checking aggression), so they may be looking for those values to collide.

Solving the Problem

Each situation will require unique solutions, but the following are some paths you might take.

☀ *Put your own feelings aside.*
Read the list of defensive reactions (above) again. Pay attention to the ones you may be feeling. Do any of these make you grit your teeth or your heart beat faster? Take a deep breath and experiment with what would happen if you let go of these reactions.

☀ *Listen to the parent's description of his experience and feelings about this matter.*
Sometimes, just knowing that you are heard is enough to encourage a person to start finding solutions. "Tell me about when you leave for school. Does taking the toy along make it easier?"

☀ *Be prepared for parents to sound tense, angry, or frustrated.*
This is probably even harder for them to deal with than it is for you. Even if they are hurtful or blaming, remember that the situation is the problem right now, not you.

☀ *Reflect back the parent's concern.*
This helps a parent know that they have been heard. "It sounds like it is really tough to get Tasha going in the morning, and bringing a toy is the one thing that has been making it easier."

☀ *Share your experience of the child at school with the parent.*
It helps for the parent to know what effect the issue has on her child's happiness at school. "What I have seen is that the toy is making it harder for Tasha to enjoy her day at school. There is so much squabbling over the toy, Tasha spends most of play time worrying about that and doesn't

take part in all of the other activities we have here in the preschool. I hate to see her missing out."

※ *Find a solution everyone is willing to try.*
Perhaps Tasha loves dogs. Maybe if you had some toy dogs in the block area, she wouldn't feel the need to bring her stuffed dogs from home. Maybe she wants her friends to see her toy and bringing a photo or drawing of the toy will suffice. Maybe she needs to bring a piece of home with her to school to feel safe, and putting the toy up on a shelf or in her cubby until she leaves will be good enough. Maybe she just needs the reassurance of walking out the door of her home with something familiar and can leave it in the car with her parent.

After the Problem Is Solved: Moving Toward True Partnership

You can address each issue as it comes up, or you can stretch yourself and your policies to partner with families. The following are some ideas of places to start.

※ *Work with parents to create policies based on a shared vision of a desirable classroom environment.*
At a parent meeting early in the year, have a brainstorming session about the physical and emotional atmosphere, and how a good environment can be created.

※ *Stay open to alternatives.*
For instance, well-known preschool teacher Bev Bos allows children to bring an item from home and drop it in a basket for "showing." At the appropriate time, children are invited to retrieve their item and can show it to a friend. This gives children the opportunity to show their friends toys from home without subjecting the class to the boring ritual of "Show and Tell."

Before You Have a Problem

Read through the following list and check off what you have already accomplished (see pages 32–36). If many of the checkboxes are blank, you have work to do to create an environment where problems are easy to solve.

☐ *Give parents copies of policies.*
Have both parents read the policy? Maybe dad (or mom) didn't know toys were not allowed.

☐ *Write policies clearly.*
Is it clear what is not allowed? Maybe parents think a "learning game," such as a portable computer game, is a different category from a toy.

☐ *Talk to parents about policies during enrollment.*
Go over this rule when the child enrolls. Parents have a lot to focus on when reading through a parent handbook, and they may not have noticed a particular rule. Once children start bringing toys, it is more uncomfortable for everyone to change the routine.

☐ *Compromise and stay flexible whenever possible.*
If you aren't willing to consider alternatives, you are missing an opportunity to model problem solving in child rearing for the parent.

☐ *Avoid judgments about parents' concerns or disagreements with policies.*
Think about the language you use in your policies. "Superheroes and other violent toys" is a judgment. Some people think that superheroes are good role models for children.

☐ *Understand parents' concern for their child's happiness.*
Making their child cry to abide by a rule they don't understand or agree with isn't going to feel okay to most parents.

Scenario 2: Fear of Health Problems Part 1, or, The Sun Devil

Emma thinks that Kenny's mom is overreacting:

> "Mrs. Keller told us that Kenny is sensitive to the sun and that he should wear a hat outdoors. That's fine, but I don't want to be the Hat Police. She said he doesn't mind wearing the hat but I should remind him. I always make sure he puts it on before we go on the playground, but it tends to fall off. I want children to be physically active. Kenny isn't the most coordinated kid. If he is worrying about his hat, he's not paying attention to climbing and running.
>
> The other day Mrs. Keller came when we were on the playground and she just went off on me about Kenny not wearing his hat. Doesn't she realize I have nineteen other children to think about? I need to make sure no one really gets hurt outdoors. Making Kenny wear his hat is not my first priority."

For Mrs. Keller, it is a very big deal:

> "I don't know why Kenny's teacher won't have him wear his hat! He is only three years old and can't be expected to know he has to wear a hat. My dad died of skin cancer and Kenny is predisposed to have sun sensitivity. I bought him a hat he likes just for day care. I don't have any trouble getting him to wear his hat at home, but when the kids are outside when I pick Kenny up, he never has his hat on! How hard can it be? I can't go to work and keep my mind on my job if I think that Kenny isn't getting what he needs."

What Is the Problem?

Health issues cut to the core of parenting. What makes parents fearful may be less related to actual danger and more related to past experiences. You cannot talk a parent out of a health-related fear unless you are a physician or mental health counselor. This is true for fears related to allergies, exposure to communicable disease, and injury. The best you can do is to be flexible when you can, and be clear about limits when changes would have a negative effect on the program.

If a parent is upset because a child experiences a health-related problem at school or the parent perceives that you have placed the child at risk, information and levelheadedness are the most valuable ways of keeping the problem from escalating.

Document, document, document! It is very upsetting to be second-guessed when you believe you acted appropriately in a crisis. Keeping records of what happened will serve you. Sometimes parents seem accepting about an event and days later appear angry or accusing about actions taken. This may be a function of the parent calming down and moving beyond initial relief that nothing worse happened, or sometimes the other parent has a different reaction.

What Are You Thinking?

Be aware of how your reaction might make the situation worse. It is easier to move into finding positive solutions if you can avoid getting into the following mind-sets, recognizing them as unhelpful to developing a healthy partnership with parents. Typical defensive reactions include these:

☀ *"This parent doesn't trust me!"*
   When a parent fears for her child's safety, even a spouse may be scrutinized. It is not about you—it's about the child.

☀ *"This parent's demands will keep me from being able to perform my job for the other children."*
   Remember that it isn't reasonable to expect parents to care as much about the well-being of other children as the well-being of their own child.

☀ *"What if something really bad happens?"*
   It is always possible that a child will be injured in some way while in group care, which is one of the consequences of dealing with such a vulnerable population. Restricting your program to only healthy children without known problems won't keep you safe.

What Are They Thinking?

Concerns over health are especially prevalent with parents of children with special needs.

☀ *"The teacher isn't taking good care of my child."*
   When a child experiences a serious illness, the parents are often overwhelmed by a sense of powerlessness. They can become determined to keep anything bad from happening to their child again. Children with chronic health problems have stronger reactions to seemingly innocuous exposures, such as common childhood diseases or insect bites, than other children and may require greater vigilance.

☀ *"The teacher isn't telling me what is really happening at school."*
Keep parents informed about near misses. Your initial reaction to a crisis
avoided (such as a child almost receiving the wrong dose of medicine at
school or a child falling from a tree but landing on the grass) might be
to want to put it out of your mind, but rumors have a way of spreading.
If children tell their parents about an event, they are likely to get parts of
it wrong. If parents have first heard about the event from you, they can
fill in the blanks to the stories they hear from their child. Meet with a
parent after an event to analyze what happened. Is it likely to happen
again? Some problems are difficult to avoid (such as a birthday treat
from home with ingredients that some children are allergic to). Having a
plan for what will happen next time is valuable. It lets parents know that
you understand their need to have a say in what happens to their child
when out of their care. It also tells parents that you take the problem seriously enough to spend time talking about it.

Solving the Problem

Each situation will require unique solutions, but the following are some
paths you might take.

☀ *Put your own feelings aside.*
This is not about you. Annoyance at having to keep track of a hat is not
the same level of emotion as being afraid your child will contract skin
cancer.

☀ *Listen to the parent's description of his experience and feelings about this
matter.*
It is hard to resist defensiveness, but it helps if you keep your attention
on the parent.

☀ *Be prepared for parents to sound tense, angry, or frustrated.*
Sometimes scared sounds like angry so resist reaction to the parent's
comments.

☀ *Reflect back the parent's concern.*
This is when you can really show the parent you get it. "It must be hard
to live in this climate and worry about your son being in danger!"

☀ *Share your experience of the child at school with the parent.*
"I now understand the importance of Kenny wearing a hat but I want to
figure out a way for him to be really active at school. When he slows
down because his hat is coming loose, he is not taking part in the active
play that is so good for his motor development."

☀ *Find a solution everyone is willing to try.*
Can your group use the playground earlier in the day when the sun is
less intense? Can you find hats that stay on more easily? Would a hat
that Kenny chose be easier for him to remember? Can you make Kenny
feel part of the group by reading *Caps for Sale* and having hats for everyone to use?

After the Problem Is Solved: Moving Toward True Partnership

You can address each issue as it comes up, or you can stretch yourself and
your policies to partner with families. The following are places to start.

☀ *Invite parents to talk to each other.*
A buddy system for parents whose children have similar issues can be
helpful and welcoming. If you have a child entering your program with
peanut allergies, ask a veteran family with peanut issues to call the parents and talk to them.

☀ *Have parents perform an audit.*
Invite a parent of a child with health issues to evaluate how the program
handles the issue, including policies, supplies, training, and so on. It can
give you useful information and help create trust with the parent.

Before You Have a Problem

Read through the following list and check off what you have already accomplished (see pages 32–36). If many of the checkboxes are blank, you have
work to do to solve problems and create an environment where problems
are easy to solve.

☐ *Make program policies consistent with laws and rules that affect your
program.*
If this child has a health issue, you may be obligated by the ADA to take
all reasonable precautions to protect him from the sun. Be clear about
your limits. For instance, you may be able to exclude rabbits from a particular classroom if a child has an allergy, but unable to ban rabbits from
the entire school.

☐ *Tell parents about policies before enrollment.*
Talk to parents before children enroll in your program about their
concerns. Ask lots of questions to be sure you understand the level of
concern. "Do you want him wearing a hat even if it's cloudy?" Or for
an allergic child: "If your child is stung by a bee do you want us to call
you even if she seems fine?" "What first aid are you expecting us to

administer?" Have a plan for what will happen if the child has a health incident at school. Go beyond just filling out the emergency card. Talk to the parent about who should be called first and under what circumstances, and about what should happen if you're on a field trip.

☐ *Compromise and stay flexible whenever possible.*
If it's going to be hard to walk on a windy day while wearing a hat, make a plan with the parent for alternative sun protection. Use clear language. Avoid phrases such as, *rarely, occasionally,* and *often.* They mean different things to different people. Try to use numbers (twice a week, once a day) so parents know what you mean.

☐ *Avoid judgments about parents' concerns or disagreements with politics.*
It is not up to you to determine if this child is truly in danger. That is the task of his parents and doctors.

☐ *Understand parents' concern for their child's happiness.*
Try to make it easy for parents to insist on consistency between home and school. It is possible to give a child the unintended message that you don't think he should have to follow his mother's rule.

. . . .

Scenario 3: Fear of Health Problems Part 2, or, Typhoid Mary

Betsy is feeling defensive:

"Everyone knows that part of being in preschool is getting colds and other bugs. We have rules, and the parents basically follow them but kids still get sick. Most of the parents are really understanding about it but Mrs. Lewis gets really upset. She only sends her son to child care on Tuesdays, and she calls every Wednesday to say he is sick again, as if it's our fault. I don't know what she expects us to do!"

Mrs. Lewis has her own perspective:

"I do my best to keep my son out of child care because I know how sick kids get. Relatives watch him almost every day but I have to send him in on Tuesdays. Every time I drop him off I see kids with runny noses, who are coughing and just not looking healthy. I tell my son to stay away from them but he always gets sick. I don't know if they won't make parents keep their kids home because they don't want to lose the money, or what. I think it would help if they kept the place cleaner, too. I wouldn't worry so much but he always has ear infections, and the pediatrician says it will affect his language development."

What Is the Problem?

Having a sick child turns a parent's life upside down. Parents worry about their child and hate seeing their child uncomfortable. Alternate child care arrangements must be made or parents must miss work. Children who don't feel well tend to not sleep well, which affects parents' sleep. Add to this fear about how infections can affect children's development and guilt over placing a child in harm's way, if child care is where they get sick. Even if children are not picking up illnesses at school, parents are likely to assume it is the culprit.

Once a parent has become upset over exposure to illness, remind them of your safety practices. Listen to their frustration with patience. If they have suggestions for improvement of your policies, listen politely so parents will feel heard. Saying, "Those are some interesting ideas. I'll give them some thought," doesn't commit you to anything.

If procedures have not been followed, let the parent know that you are aware of what happened and that steps will be taken to ensure that it won't happen again.

What Are You Thinking?

Be aware of how your reaction might make the situation worse. It is easier to move into finding positive solutions if you can avoid getting into the following mind-sets, recognizing them as unhelpful to developing a healthy partnership with parents. Typical defensive reactions include these:

☀ *"This parent doesn't think the school is clean."*
People have different standards for sanitation, and you are likely to have some parents in the program who would prefer a more hospital-like level of cleanliness. It isn't about you as a person.

☀ *"This parent will say bad things about the program to her pediatrician and we'll get a bad reputation."*
Most doctors understand the issues of exposure in group child care.

☀ *"This parent expects you to handle her child with kid gloves."*
It is important to keep any conflict with parents from interfering with your relationship with the child. Resist the urge to pull away from the child emotionally.

What Are Parents Thinking?

☀ *"My child is going to pick up something terrible!"*
Some cultures fuss over health more than others.

☀ *"How can I afford to take her to the doctor again?"*
Parents with limited access to health care will be especially concerned about illness.

☀ *"I'm going to miss work again. I hope I don't lose my job!"*
Parents in minimum-wage jobs or jobs without benefits are hurt by loss of pay when staying home with a sick child.

Solving the Problem

Each situation will require unique solutions, but the following are some paths you might take.

☀ *Put your own feelings aside.*
Parents don't have as much experience with typical childhood illnesses as most teachers. We may groan when we have a lice outbreak, but for parents it can be exhausting and humiliating.

☀ *Reflect back the parent's concern.*
"It sounds like taking your child to the doctor means a long bus ride and a day's pay lost. I can see how hard that is."

☀ *Share your experience of the child at school with the parent.*
"I know it's scary when your child has a fever. But when you keep her home because you are afraid she might get sick, it's hard for her to develop relationships with the other children. Adjustment has to start all over again."

☀ *Find a solution everyone is willing to try.*
I worked with several children who were undergoing chemotherapy. It was always a delicate balance trying to limit their exposure to illness and ensure a consistent school experience. Parents were willing to write a note to the other parents in the class asking to call them at home if their child had been exposed to something that would not be serious for a healthy child but placed the child with a compromised immune system in jeopardy. Parents were happy to comply and also tended to be more cautious about sending a sick child to school.

After the Problem Is Solved: Moving Toward True Partnership

You can address each issue as it comes up, or you can stretch yourself and your policies to partner with families. The following are some places to start.

☀ *Invite a public health nurse to a parent meeting.*
A public health nurse could inform parents about disease exposure in child care settings.

☀ *Invite parents to take part in an audit.*
Ask parents to help evaluate the health and safety policies and procedures and to make suggestions for improvement.

☀ *Encourage parents to spend time in the program.*
When parents realize the benefits for their child in taking part in the program, they may be less concerned about the occasional cold.

Before You Have Problems

Read through the following list and check off what you have already accomplished (see pages 32–36). If many of the checkboxes are blank, you have work to do to solve problems and create an environment where problems are easy to solve.

☐ *Make program policies consistent with laws and rules that affect your program.*
Most programs are licensed by a state agency and rules about contagious diseases are usually included. National Association for the Education of Young Children accreditation also addresses this topic.

Make sure your policies are consistent with these rules as well as with the best current pediatric health information. Be sure that the staff is using sound health practices. Have all children and adults wash their hands as soon as they enter the building. This can help keep germs out. Teach adults and children sanitary hand-washing procedures, including using a paper towel to turn off the faucet, which guards against picking up germs that have been left behind. Sanitize toys often. Avoid sharing bottles or food.

☐ *Give parents copies of policies.*
It is often helpful to give parents a separate flier to keep at home that tells when children must stay home from school. A parent isn't likely to think about rashes or lice until they have the experience. Be clear about refund policies for when children miss school. You don't want to have an argument with a parent who is already stressed out over having a sick child.

☐ *Write policies clearly.*
When must a child be kept at home? Make sure the policy is specific (a temperature of over 100 degrees) rather than general (with a fever).

☐ *Make consequences of not following policies clear.*
What happens if a child comes to school sick? What happens if a child does not attend school regularly? Spell it out.

☐ *Tell parents about policies before enrollment.*
Help parents understand that their children are taking part in a larger germ pool by attending school. It can help to point out to parents that they can either expose their children to typical childhood germs now or wait until they enter elementary school when absence from school affects their child's academic experience differently.

Talk to parents about arrangements for children who become ill when they first enroll their children. Have a specific location for isolating sick children. Include a system for notifying parents if children need to be picked up from school. Make sure they have names of people other than the parents themselves. If the backups are out of town or unavailable, you can be stuck until pickup time. Send out notices of exposure. While it might seem overwhelming to tell every parent about every exposure, they usually appreciate having a heads-up.

☐ *Compromise and stay flexible whenever possible.*
Hear what parents would like you to do to cut back on exposures and consider their suggestions.

☐ *Avoid judgments about parent's concerns or disagreements with policies.*
A simple cold may seem like no big deal to you, but it can have a huge
effect on a family, ranging from lost sleep to lost work and medical bills.

☐ *Understand parents' concern for their child's happiness.*
A parent is naturally going to be most concerned with his own child's
health. Saying to another parent, "I know that other child has a nasty
cough but he's missed so much school. I just hated to send him home
again," will not be an acceptable response for most parents.

☐ *Develop relationships.*
Encourage parents to spend time in the program. When parents realize
the benefits for their child in taking part in the program, they will be less
concerned about the occasional cold.

....

Scenario 4: The Parent Who Won't Leave, or, "How can I miss you when you won't say good-bye?"

Tommy's teacher is ready for his mom to move on:

> "Tommy's mom is making him miserable! She just won't leave! We have a whole routine of two kisses and two hugs; then the teacher holds his hand when mom leaves. She just keeps prolonging it. He cries and she comes back. We start the whole cycle over again. She leaves and realizes she forgot to check his cubby. Or she decides she has to tell me something. Each time she comes back, he gets upset all over again. This keeps me tied up for an hour every morning, and it's time I can't spend with the other children."

Tommy's mom is struggling:

> "It's just so hard to leave Tommy. I try to put on a happy face, and I begin each morning telling him how much fun he is going to have at school. But then we get there, and when I try to leave, he cries and cries. His teacher just expects me to leave him crying. It's too hard! I don't want him to feel abandoned. I know it's taking a long time but he is just too upset. You can tell she isn't a parent and doesn't know how it feels to leave your child crying."

What Is the Problem?

Separation is a huge deal for parents. While we as teachers have seen children making this transition every year and can predict how long it's going to take, it is a very personal issue for parents. Guilt over leaving the child, fear of leaving the child in the "wrong hands," fear of losing the child's love and trust, sadness at missing one's child, and personal issues of abandonment and loss—all play into the intensity. By bullying parents to move through this issue at our pace we risk forcing the parents to sabotage the adjustment efforts or to give up some of their self-image as parents. Neither is good for children.

What Are You Thinking?

Be aware of how your reaction might make the situation worse. It is easier to move into finding positive solutions if you can avoid getting into the following mind-sets, recognizing them as unhelpful to developing a healthy partnership with parents. Typical defensive reactions include these:

☀ *"If I let the child manipulate me he will be less compliant."*
While it is important for children to accept routines and limits, separation anxiety is real (Balaban 1985). Very few children use it for manipulation. If you stop questioning the sincerity of the child's feelings, it is easier to find a good solution.

☀ *"If I let the parent break the rules, she won't accept my authority."*
The best way to avoid this issue is to avoid inflexible rules.

☀ *"I am losing control of my classroom with all of these parents hanging around."*
Some teachers thrive in an environment full of adults. Others are overwhelmed by having many bodies and personalities in the classroom. You can adjust your schedule so that "serious" things happen after the parents leave. I have also set limits for parents if I felt they were becoming their children's school playmates and interfering with their children adjusting to the teacher and other children. I have said, "You need to be present so your child feels secure but not interesting enough that they depend on you to navigate the classroom. Be boring. Sit in the same chair. Bring a magazine or some work." I have then slowly moved the chair toward the classroom door, into the hall, into the entryway, and eventually out the door.

☀ *"The other parents are going to think they should stay too."*
You can reassure other parents that their children are fine with the parent leaving.

☀ *"The parent must think I can't handle her child."*
This is probably not the case. If it is, you can help the parent change her mind by observing you with other children.

☀ *"The parent is going to observe me doing things he won't approve of."*
Most parents in this situation will be so focused on their own child that they won't judge the teacher. There is a risk that the parent will observe things they don't understand and report information to other parents. All you can do is trust other parents to read through the situation.

☀ *"The child will never bond with me."*
Take steps to develop a rapport with the child. Don't depend on the parent to handle her child in the classroom and the bonding will happen faster.

☀ *"I am spending so much time with this child, the other children aren't getting my attention."*
In general, all of the children in the group are relieved that the teacher is caring for an anxious friend and are not jealous. If you find that the separation transition is taking so long that it is interfering with your

interactions with other children, you can arrange for parents to let you know when they are ready for help leaving and focus on the other children until then.

What Are Parents Thinking?

☀ *"This teacher doesn't understand how my people feel about a mother leaving her child."*
Separation is a culturally sensitive issue. It is important that you understand the cultural norms of the groups you serve. Are mothers supposed to stay with their children? They may not say this to you, in an attempt to fit in with the dominant culture, but mothers may be torn between your expectation that they leave and their culture's expectation that they stay with their children. If you expect more independence from children than their culture demands, mothers may feel that their children will not be properly cared for. Examples include expectations for self-feeding and being carried by an adult.

☀ *"The teacher doesn't understand how boys are supposed to act."*
Expectations may be different for boys than for girls. If boys are expected not to cry, it may be difficult for a parent to leave their child in tears. Divisions between the expectations of fathers and of mothers create a lack of consistency and add to adjustment difficulties.

☀ *"The teacher's wrong. I'm just going to do what is right for my child."*
Communication styles are an issue. Parents may not approve of the separation policy and may not tell you. In some cultures, it is rude to disagree with people. So parents may verbally agree to an action but not follow through.

☀ *"The teacher says he stops crying as soon as I leave, but how can I be sure?"*
Trust is an issue. If you are different from a family in culture, language, or in other ways, you may not be trusted to care for their children once they leave. Parents bring their own childhood experiences into their roles as parents. If a parent is not allowed to use his native language in school or if he experiences favoritism of one group over another, it may take a while for you to earn his trust.

Solving the Problem

Each situation will require unique solutions, but the following are some paths you might take.

☀ *Put your own feelings aside.*
Once you find yourself in a power struggle with a parent about leaving the classroom, stop before it escalates and have a meeting. Make a plan together.

☀ *Listen to the parent's description of her experience and feelings.*
Evaluate the present situation. Listen to the parent. While the parent may feel she is making progress with her child or says, "This is how it always is when I leave," you may find the situation is detrimental to the child or the other children.

☀ *Share your experience of the child at school with the parent.*
Share what you are seeing in an objective way. Saying, "You never leave," is emotionally loaded. Try, "You say good-bye and then stay for ten to twenty minutes." Saying, "Each time you come back, Tommy cries and has a bad day," is guilt inducing. Try, "Tommy takes up to an hour before he joins in activity and wakes up from nap crying."

☀ *Find a solution everyone is willing to try.*
Get some history. How has the child dealt with separation? What was traumatic? What went easily? Brainstorm some ideas with the parent. Make a plan that you can both live with. Compromise may be required. You may think it would be easier if the parent brought the child to school earlier, when there are fewer children for you to attend to. If she is not able or willing to do this, you need to move on to a new idea. Ask the parent to describe what the ideal scenario would look like. Would the child run into the classroom and not look back? Would he hug mom and then turn to the arms of his teacher? Find out if you both have the same image so you will have a common goal. Plan a script together. Come up with signals that show the parent is ready for you to take the child from her arms. It will be easiest for the child to see you working as a united front.

☀ *Decide together what success will look like.*
Prepare the parent for setbacks. Try to get a commitment to work on a plan over a period of time. Let the parent know that regression is common, especially if circumstances change—such as a parent going out of town or having a substitute teacher at school. Celebrate small steps toward success. When the parent can leave for a portion of the day, that's a step. When the child stops crying a few minutes after the parent leaves, that's a step.

After the Problem Is Solved: Moving Toward True Partnership

You can address each issue as it comes up, or you can stretch yourself and your policies to partner with families. The following are some places to start:

☀ Create a "good-bye window" or other physical place for families to separate.

☀ Provide parents with a way to view their children that is out of sight, such as two-way mirrors or a video camera they can check from work.

Before You Have a Problem

Read through the following list and check off what you have already accomplished (see pages 32–36). If many of the checkboxes are blank, you have work to do to create an environment where problems are easy to solve.

☐ *Make program policies consistent with laws and rules that affect your program.*
When laws do not address this issue, you can still look to best practices in the early childhood education field. Will you have different rules for different ages of children? Do you expect the same from parents of infants and toddlers as you do for preschoolers or schoolagers? Think through policies for developmental appropriateness.

☐ *Write policies clearly.*
How long are you willing to let parents stay? It can be helpful to state up front how long you will proceed with a plan and when you will review it together. This keeps you from sticking with a plan that is obviously not working and sets the tone that you will work through issues with the parent as a team.

☐ *Make consequences of not following policies clear.*
What is your bottom line with separation? At what point is it not working? Do you believe someone is to blame if a child does not make a successful transition into your program? When I was a young teacher, I had an insightful parent say to me after a couple of weeks of trying to get her son to separate, "Right now Matthew is an oval peg and school is a round hole. I feel like if I pushed and prodded hard enough, I'd get him in the space, but it won't be comfortable or natural. Let's wait another year and see what shape he takes." She was absolutely right, and the next year he made an easy transition. It was lucky that she had the luxury of allowing him another year before starting school.

☐ *Talk to parents about policies at enrollment.*
How do you define successful separation and adjustment? Talk to the parents before enrollment. They may expect that their child will not cry, and it won't seem successful to them until they leave with no tears. They may expect the child to be engaged in play before they leave. This can lead to a vicious cycle of a parent coaxing the child to engage in activity only to find the child disengages when the parent attempts to leave. The parent may expect the child to choose to have the parent leave and won't leave until the child approves the move. This places too much responsibility on the child.

☐ *Compromise and stay flexible whenever possible.*
Having a policy that provides flexibility for different situations and individuals will be easiest to enforce and the most useful in the long run.

☐ *Avoid judgments about parents' concerns or disagreements with policies.*
Teachers often make this comment, "It's not the child who is having a hard time. His mom is just encouraging him to cry!" For young children, the connection between parent and child is so strong, the origin of the concern doesn't matter.

☐ *Understand parents' concern for their child's happiness.*
Share information, such as the National Association for the Education of Young Children's brochure, "So Many Goodbyes," so parents know they are not alone.

☐ *Develop a relationship.*
Acknowledging the challenges of separation is a good place to start developing a partnership. Encourage supportive parents to help each other by planning to arrive at school at the same time so the child can walk in with a buddy.

. . . .

Scenario 5: The Late Parent, or, "Is it 6:15 already?"

Dora has had it!

> "Mimi's dad is always late. I've tried to be subtle, looking at the clock a lot, saying, 'Oh, Mimi, your dad is finally here!' But he doesn't get the hint. When he finally does come she is so wound up from waiting for him that she runs around the room, making him chase her. Then they play this game while I am trying to leave! It's bad enough he is ten minutes late, but then by the time he gets her, signs her out, gets stuff out of her cubby, has her go potty one more time, it's more like a half an hour. My director says she can't charge him when he is just ten minutes late, but I am getting out of work a half hour late every night!"

Mimi's father has a totally different read on the situation:

> "Mimi's teacher doesn't seem to care much about her work. She just seems to care about punching the clock and leaving. I've tried chatting with her when I pick up Mimi, but she's not very friendly. It's my only opportunity to see what Mimi's school is like, since her mom drops her off in the morning. I never hear about Mimi's day, and if I try to read notices on the parent bulletin board or look at the kids' art work, the teacher tries to get me to leave."

What Is the Problem?

For many parents, the program's closing time means the time they need to get there. If a store closes at 5:00 P.M., they will still let you shop and ring you out as long as you get in the door on time. Parents may feel guilty about the long hours they are away from their child and want to show an interest in their classroom when they arrive. It may not occur to them that the teacher is anxious to leave. This can be especially challenging to understand for parents who have jobs without set hours.

What Are You Thinking?

Be aware of how your reaction might make the situation worse. It is easier to move into finding positive solutions if you can avoid getting into the following mind-sets, recognizing them as unhelpful to developing a healthy partnership with parents. Typical defensive reactions include these:

☀ *"This parent thinks I am her personal babysitter."*
It is easy to feel marginalized by families who seem oblivious to your
need to leave work on time. There are many explanations for a parent
who does not adhere to pickup time, so don't personalize it.

☀ *"If I let them come late without consequences, they'll continue to take advantage of me."*
It is difficult for some of us to stand up for our own rights. Have faith
that you and the parent can solve the problem together. The parent is
probably not deliberately taking advantage of you.

☀ *"These parents think they are above the rules."*
It can be hard to watch some parents work so hard to get to school on
time and others not bother. Try not to make generalizations that will
have a negative impact on your relationship.

What Are Parents Thinking?

☀ *"Why is this teacher so uptight about time?"*
Time is a concept bound by culture. While stereotypes about ethnic
groups being late are disrespectful, adherence to the clock is a Western-
European concept. Instead of assuming negative reasons for parents
being habitually late, it is helpful to think instead of a different notion of
what "on time" might mean.

Solving the Problem

Each situation will require unique solutions, but the following are some
paths you might take:

☀ *Put your own feelings aside.*
Keep the issue from clouding your relationship with the family. It is easy
for a frustration such as this to become the center of the relationship between a teacher and parent. The biggest losers are the children. This is
not the child's fault and is probably just one aspect in the interaction between the school and parent.

☀ *Listen to the parent's description of his experience and feelings about this matter.*
You may find that the parents are struggling with pickup time as much
as you are.

☀ *Reflect back the parent's concern.*
"It sounds like you can't get here with more than five minutes to spare
and then you don't get a chance to see the classroom."

☀ *Share your experience with the parent and how it affects the child at school.*
Help the parent understand the consequence for his child. "When Ethan is the last child to get picked up, he gets anxious. I know that isn't how you want to start your evening with him."

☀ *Find a solution everyone is willing to try.*
You can brainstorm with parents to find a solution. Include suggesting a carpool with another family, having the family hire a teaching assistant to stay late with the child, or meeting the family in the parking lot with the child. If you take the position of partnering with the family to solve this problem rather than taking an adversarial position, you will win the co-operation of the family in other matters. Have children ready to go. If parents have to spend ten minutes finding their children's shoes, you are going to get out even later. Having children all ready is another signal that it is time to go. Help parents out the door. Sometimes children react to waiting for a late parent by trying to make the parent wait for them. Help the parent herd the child out, assuring the child that there will be time to show her work to her parent or finish that game tomorrow.

After the Problem Is Solved: Moving Toward True Partnership

You can address each issue as it comes up, or you can stretch yourself and your policies to partner with families. The following are some places to start.

☀ *Find out what parents need.*
Maybe polling parents will tell you they need you to add more hours to your program.

☀ *Find out about transportation services.*
Some communities have bus services that parents can use.

Before You Have Problems

Read through the following list and check off what you have already accomplished (see pages 32–36). If many of the checkboxes are blank, you have work to do to solve problems and create an environment where problems are easy to solve.

☐ *Give parents copies of policies.*
Be clear about expectations for pickup. It is helpful to have the information in several places, such as in the parent handbook, posters in the classroom, and notes sent home. If dad usually picks up, mom may not know what pick-up time is.

☐ *Make policies.*
Don't give double messages. If parents apologize for being late and you tell them "no big deal," they are less likely to rush next time. Be polite but clear about the need for parents to come on time.

☐ *Make consequences of not following policies clear.*
Have a policy in place that deters late pickup. Most programs have a late fee. If possible, involve an administrator in the issue so it does not turn into a power struggle between you and the parent. You might waive the fee the first time it happens and state, "This time we'll waive the fee, but next time we'll have to charge you." This way, parents leave feeling relieved and understand the consequence for being late.

☐ *Pay attention to the details.*
Make sure clocks in the school are synchronized and accurate. The issue may be differing watches.

Scenario 6: The Parent Who Wants Special Treatment, or, "If it's not too much trouble . . ."

Antonia doesn't understand this parent's expectations:

> "Ryan's mom always wants something special. He can't eat our hot lunches because the family is vegetarian. I respect that. But she brings food she wants us to heat up for him. That means I have to leave the classroom to use the microwave in the kitchen. Other teachers, who are on break, are heating up their own lunches so I have to wait for them to finish. In the meantime, I have left my teaching assistant alone in the classroom to help all the other children with lunch. I've asked the mom to bring food that doesn't have to be heated, and she'll do that for a couple of days, but then we are back to the microwave again."

Ryan's mom is focused on her son's experience:

> "It is hard for Ryan to be the only one in his class that eats different food. You should see the garbage they feed the kids—hot dogs and other foods full of chemicals and all kinds of things. I explained that we are vegetarians and we would bring food for Ryan each day when I enrolled him. The administration said I still had to pay the same tuition and I agreed, so they are making money on us. His teacher wants us to send cheese sandwiches every day so her life is easier, but I want Ryan to feel like the other kids. I look at their menu and try to fix him something similar like veggie burgers. The other kids are getting hot food, why shouldn't Ryan?"

What Is the Problem?

The teacher may view the eating habits of the family as a choice and the family does not see it as a choice. Food issues are not that different from other diversity issues. If you are Christian, you may not notice how many holidays and events are based on Christian culture. If you are not Christian, you are always aware of when your religious traditions are different from the majority culture. The same can be true for families who eat differently. While the teacher sees the parent as making special demands, from the perspective of the parent, if all of the children were fed "properly," it wouldn't be an issue. If a power struggle emerges over this issue, take a step back and focus on a solution that will work for everyone rather than trying to win.

What Are You Thinking?

Be aware of how your reaction might make the situation worse. It is easier to move into finding positive solutions if you can avoid getting into the following mind-sets, recognizing them as unhelpful to developing a healthy partnership with parents. Typical defensive reactions include these:

☀ *"I am just supporting this parent's eccentricity."*
Diets can be based on religion, beliefs around health or politics (some people are vegetarians because it takes less land to grow vegetables than to feed cows), personal preference, or spiritual reasons (sometimes diets are designed by spiritual healers). If you try to judge a parent's reasons for making such choices, you are stepping over a line.

☀ *"If I give into this, the parent will have a new demand."*
No one wants to be taken advantage of. Still, children are part of their families. Addressing families' needs is part of working well with children.

What Are Parents Thinking?

☀ *"The teacher doesn't support my decisions about my child."*
As stated above, religion or culture can dictate diet. Refusing to cooperate with these exceptions can signal a lack of tolerance for differences.

Solving the Problem

Each situation will require unique solutions, but the following are some paths you might take.

☀ *Be clear about the issue.*
If the parent's request is a problem, be clear about the issue. Is it accommodating a vegetarian? Is it food from home? Is it preparing the food? The solution to the dilemma depends on why it is a problem. If you cannot accommodate a vegetarian, then you are not going to make an inviting school for people from some countries and cultures.

☀ *Find a solution everyone is willing to try.*
If leaving the room is the problem, maybe the parents can donate a microwave to the classroom. If the issue is food from home, it might be time to look at your menu. If you come up with a solution (such as having the parents bring food that does not need heating) and the parents don't follow through, immediately contact them for a new solution. You can't let the child go hungry, but you could keep crackers and peanut butter in your classroom and inform the parent you didn't have time to leave the room so you substituted the food.

After the Problem Is Solved: Moving Toward True Partnership

You can address each issue as it comes up, or you can stretch yourself and your policies to partner with families. The following are places to start:

❄ *Show support for families who differ from the dominant culture.*
Include the needs of these families in school policies.

❄ *Why not serve only vegetarian food?*
Vegetarian meals won't hurt anyone and would be a great show of support for vegetarian families.

❄ *Find out if all the parents would be just as happy to send lunches from home.*
You may be jumping through hoops for no reason.

Before You Have Problems

Read through the following list and check off what you have already accomplished (see pages 32–36). If many of the checkboxes are blank, you have work to do to create an environment where problems are easy to solve.

☐ *Make program policies consistent with laws and rules that affect your program.*
If your program receives subsidies from the United States Department of Agriculture, you must meet specific standards about what children are served in order to use them in the counts. Menus need to be reevaluated every so often. We now have different standards for healthy diets than we did when the food pyramid first came out and some of us have too many saturated fats in our menus.

☐ *Give parents copies of policies.*
Giving parents written menus and making sure to update menus gives parents a sense of security.

☐ *Write policies clearly.*
Make sure this is a part of the enrollment procedure so problems don't come up later. Menus must be clear. For instance, chili may have meat, beans, or both. Making recipes available for parents is helpful.

☐ *Compromise and stay flexible whenever possible.*
Establish similarities between home and school. When populations change (for example, families from different countries), it can be beneficial to reevaluate the school lunches. Parents can be helpful in evaluating menu changes. Ask questions about food before the child begins. If parents have special requests, make a plan to honor them.

☐ *Avoid judgments about parents' concerns or disagreements with policies.*
Keep an open mind about the solution. Be aware of your own prejudices.
I worked with one teacher who objected to a parent substituting a rice
cake for the wheat crackers her child was allergic to, saying, "The rice
cake is so big, it doesn't seem fair." Chances are, the other children are
not going to care about what others eat if they know there is a reason.

· ·

Scenario 7: The Child with Special Needs, or, "Why didn't you tell us?"

Eric is concerned:

"I always interview parents before they enroll their children to see if there is anything we should know. We even ask for developmental history. So Sean starts in my class, and I have no idea he has issues. Right away I can tell something is wrong. During free play he is fine—he likes to use the blocks and finds a place where he can play without other children bothering him. But he hates clean-up time. When I sing the clean-up song, he gets excited, flapping his arms. I give him instructions, and he repeats back what I say. I tried physically moving him to the shelf to put away blocks. He started pushing me away and screamed. Now I just avoid the whole thing by letting him play with blocks through group time and snack time. I don't know what else to do. I also feel angry with his mother for not telling me he was like this."

Sean's parent is trying to protect him:

"Sean's teacher is having a hard time working with him. He has always been sensitive, but as long as you tell him what is going to happen beforehand and keep to the same routine, he's fine. Lots of little kids are like that. His pediatrician said he is a little behind in some things, but I know he'll catch up. I thought this was a good school, and they'd teach him how to behave. His last school asked him to leave because they weren't good with him. I didn't mention it to the new school because I didn't want him to start off on the wrong foot. Now I feel like his teacher doesn't like him."

What Is the Problem?

Don't expect to get the whole picture from your first contact with families. The more challenging the child, the more likely parents will need to develop trust in you before divulging everything. Don't take it personally. If you do find yourself in the position of working with a child with special needs when you were not prepared to do so, move forward rather than focusing on what should have happened. Blame, second-guessing yourself, and resentment of the family will just divert your energies from finding the best solution to the dilemma.

What Are You Thinking?

Be aware of how your reaction might make the situation worse. It is easier to move into finding positive solutions if you can avoid getting into the following mind-sets, recognizing them as unhelpful to developing a healthy partnership with parents. Typical defensive reactions include these:

☀ *"I am going to get blamed for this child's problems."*
Especially in this time of accountability, it is easy to focus on covering your own tail instead of on what is best for the child. While it is important to document what you have done in case questions come up, do not let it become your primary focus.

☀ *"What else is this parent withholding?"*
Regaining trust is hard once you feel like you haven't been given all of the information you need.

What Are Parents Thinking?

☀ *"If my child has something wrong with him, he will have a terrible life."*
Different cultures respond to disabilities with more or less acceptance.

☀ *"My child will never be accepted."*
Understanding the cultural implications of both parents is important. In-laws can also play a role in acceptance.

Solving the Problem

Each situation will require unique solutions, but the following are some paths you might take.

☀ *Put your own feelings aside.*
Stay focused on the present reality of the child's experience in school. It no longer matters that it would have been better if you had known beforehand. What is working for the child? What is overly challenging? What can help the child benefit from his school experience? Let go of any negative feelings toward the parents. You need to form a team now.

☀ *Listen to the parent's description of her experience and feelings about this matter.*
Get parents in the classroom. It will help if parents can see how their child behaves in comparison to other children before you have to describe the behavior. Know what resources you have access to. It helps to know about community resources and resources the family has access to (such as health insurance).

☀ *Share your experience of the child at school with the parent.*
Make a plan to meet with the parents. Be clear that the focus is on doing
what will best meet the child's needs.

☀ *Find a solution everyone is willing to try.*
Help parents move forward. Plan time and allow energy for working with
the parents to find ways to improve this child's experiences. Be clear
about your expectations. You will need the child's parents to follow
through with decisions you make together. Look at creating forms of
communication (such as written logs, e-mails, and phone calls), and set
times for future meetings. Make a plan with the parents that moves on a
continuum of least restrictive to most restrictive involvement. Target the
most difficult times and events for the child. Is it during transitions? Try
increasing support during transitions. Ask the director to help for fifteen
minutes during the move from indoors to outdoors. Is it during field
trips? Try having a family member come to help during field trips. If
these less restrictive solutions don't work, you can move toward more restrictive solutions, such as having parents pick up the child before rest
time or keeping the child home when field trips are planned. Talk to the
parents about having the child professionally assessed. Be prepared for
hesitation on the part of the parents. We are all concerned about children's permanent records and labeling a child. While it is the responsibility of the public schools to provide screening and assessment of children
ages three to twenty-one, public health facilities or private insurance car-
riers are alternatives. This information can help you make the best plans
for the child and may provide some outside resources for your program.

After the Problem Is Solved:
Moving Toward True Partnership

You can address each issue as it comes up, or you can stretch yourself and
your policies to partner with families. The following are places to start:

☀ *Become an inclusive setting.*
If you have a positive experience including a child with special needs in
your program, you may want to become an inclusive setting. This can be
accomplished by partnering with other agencies to place children with
special needs and offer the services they require.

☀ *Use Individual Education Plans (IEPs).*
Offer IEPs to all children in your center. It's a great way of ensuring
individual appropriateness and includes families in setting goals for their
children.

Before You Have Problems

Read through the following list and check off what you have already accomplished (see pages 32–36). If many of the checkboxes are blank, you have work to do to solve the problem and create an environment where problems are easy to solve.

☐ *Make program policies consistent with laws and rules that affect your program.*
Make sure you understand your legal obligations, especially in accordance with the Americans with Disabilities Act (ADA). Programs are expected to include children and parents with disabilities unless it would cause a "direct threat" to other children or "fundamental alteration" of the program. Programs are required to make "reasonable modifications" that don't cause "undue burden." For more information, you can read "Commonly Asked Questions about Child Care Centers and the Americans with Disabilities Act" on the ADA home page (see page 113).

☐ *Write policies clearly.*
Have a clear policy about serving children with special needs. Make sure it is written down and given to all parents, such as in the parent handbook. This keeps the decisions about placement and services from being personal for the families. It also gives parents the message that you are experienced in handling these issues.

☐ *Develop relationships.*
Start communicating with parents about their child's adjustment to school from the beginning. Waiting until things are overwhelming heightens tensions.

Discussion Questions

1. How were policies developed for your program? Do they stand the test of time or are they based on people or situations that are no longer an issue?
2. What policies do parents seem to challenge the most? Do they make sense from the parents' perspective? What changes might encourage greater cooperation?
3. Is there common understanding between staff members about policies? What policies do you need to talk about as a staff?

☀ 3 ☀

Finding Common Values
between Home and School

There is no such thing as a values-free program or curriculum. Values are at the heart of all the curriculum decisions we make. Sometimes, our values are so ingrained in early childhood practices, we view them as fact and as what is good for children. We don't see that they are based on our beliefs until someone challenges them.

One of the critical roles of parents is to instill the values of their family, culture, and community in their children. This is easiest when children spend their lives in a community of like-minded people. For many parents it is impractical to restrict their children's experiences to interaction only with people of similar values. This is especially true for families who are not of the dominant culture. Many parents recognize the need for their children to succeed in the dominant culture, and they work to raise bicultural children: people who are at home in their own culture and in the culture of the dominant society. When parents make this choice, they must work hard to ensure that the values of their own culture are not lost.

Other parents may choose not to restrict their children's lives to like-minded people because they value a multicultural experience. Parents often choose to send their children to nonsectarian schools even if programs that teach their faith are accessible. While parents may not have the right to expect a program to teach their values, they do have a right to expect a program to deal with differences in values in a respectful manner.

Differences in expectations for clothing, language, physical contact, and the formality or informality of speaking to adults can all be examples of values-based conflicts:

☀ **Children's clothing**

Some programs exclude party attire or clothing that has commercial messages, such as cartoon characters. Some programs insist that specific clothing is worn, such as closed-toed shoes to protect children's feet, shorts under dresses to protect girls' modesty, or underwear to protect children's hygiene.

☀ **Language**

Programs may have rules against inappropriate language. This is a problem when families use words that aren't allowed as part of everyday speech, such as words for body parts (butt) or expressions (Oh God!).

☀ **Physical contact**

A program may have rules that are too restrictive for a family to feel at home (for example, not allowing children to kiss each other or adults or not allowing children to sit on adults' laps). Or a program may have contact that is more demonstrative than families prefer.

☀ **Adult-child relationships**

Schools often direct children to call the teachers either by their first names (informal), their last names (formal), or something in between, such as "Miss Kathy" or "Auntie." If families are uncomfortable with the titles, conflict can occur. Some families (often for cultural reasons) expect their children to address adults respectfully and insist that their child greets and responds to the teacher. A teacher may defend a child's refusal to acknowledge him as a way of putting parents at ease, but it may feel like a lack of support for family values.

Beginning with your initial contact with prospective families, you can take several steps to develop and communicate program values based on shared beliefs:

1. Focus on developing common ground.
2. Continue to develop shared understanding as new families enter your program.
3. Continue to focus on how decisions either support or compete with families' values throughout their experience with your program.

Focus on Developing Common Ground

You can begin by focusing on the principles for developing common ground in relation to values. It begins with your first contact with prospective families.

First, acknowledge to yourself that you cannot develop a values-free curriculum. Be conscious of the decisions you make and which values you are supporting with those decisions. A preschool that offers only a part-day schedule projects a value about working parents. If this is not your intention, be clear about how you can meet the needs of working parents and know that they will likely assume that you do not value the choices they've made.

Second, make sure information that goes to prospective families is detailed enough to allow them to determine if there is a good match between their values and those of the program. For example, parents can make informed choices if brochures or other materials make it clear that children are encouraged to get messy at school. Parents will not necessarily interpret pat phrases like, "sensory-based experiences," or "discovery is encouraged," to mean that children may come home covered in paint, for example.

And last, focus on the connection between program goals and curriculum decisions. If you are sure these things are consistent, it is easier for parents to predict issues that will come up. For instance, if a curriculum goal is to include families in their children's learning but you do not allow parents to assist in the classroom, your policies and goals are not in alignment.

Develop Shared Understanding with New Families

The next step is continuing to develop shared understanding as a family is entering your program. You can do this by spending time with families to learn about their values. It will be easier to figure out potential conflicts and find solutions before the child begins. We recently gave a tour of our program to a parent who commented that our bathrooms didn't seem very clean. Instead of simply reassuring her that they were cleaned twice per day (which is true), the staff member conducting the tour stopped and had a conversation about our values of independence (such as allowing children to change their own clothes even if it meant clothing strewn across the room during the process) and the mother's feelings about independence and messiness. The family chose to enroll in our program and did so with full understanding of why we do certain things rather than deciding to just tolerate a perceived flaw.

Listen to parents' beliefs and opinions with respect. It is easier to pass judgment and view beliefs that differ from our own as eccentricities. Then we don't have to think! Taking time to truly hear what parents say may give you a new perspective.

Focus on How Decisions Support Families' Values

The third step involves continued focus on how decisions support or compete with families' values throughout their experience with your program. Remember the benefits of diversity. If you respond to disagreements by becoming annoyed or angry, you will miss opportunities to increase the diversity in your program. It may be easier if everyone feels the same way, but it is much more boring!

Practice flexibility. Avoid reacting by saying, "We don't do it that way," and give yourself a chance to work with parents to invent a better way.

When Nothing Seems to Work

There are times when a family's values will not mesh with the program. If you value diversity in your program, you should try to do what you can to find compromise. You may not be able to do so if one of the following could result:

❋ **The family disagrees with legally or ethically mandated practices.**
Our job is not to tell families how to discipline their children, but if we see evidence of abuse, we must report it. This will not necessarily result in the family leaving the program. In the past, I have reported families for suspected abuse, which did not lead to pulling their children from the program. Still, you should be prepared for the possibility.

❋ **Meeting the family's expectations would result in a fundamental change in the program.**
We can expect families to roll with some changes, such as changing a lunch menu to accommodate a vegetarian family. But some changes are so dramatic that the program would cease to meet other families' expectations. For example, if the program focuses on teaching positive conflict resolution and a parent wants the teacher to allow his child to hit back, the values of the program would have to change significantly to comply. Still, it may be possible to start from a place of commonality (for example, "I know that you don't want Sam to get bullied at

school, and I don't want that either"), and make an agreement in which the parent's values and the school's values are both respected.

Ultimately, you must decide which values are worth alienating families for—or, as the saying goes, which mountains you are willing to die on. While it is hard not to view losing a family from your program as a failure, hanging on to a bad fit between a program and a family is like hanging on to a bad romance. You can grow as a professional when you consider other points of view, but ultimately you need to do what you believe is right.

Be clear about what you are not willing to give up.

Scenarios

Scenario 1: When Beliefs from Home and the Program Don't Match, or, Holidaze

Maria shares her problem:

"This is my house! When Aaron's mom placed him, she told me they were Jewish. I thought that would be a nice change of pace for our group. I asked Aaron's mom to come in and light a menorah with the kids and tell us about their holiday. But now she doesn't want me to celebrate my holiday with the children! She complains about every decoration and Christmas-related book. It's not fair for her son's holiday to be the only one that is acknowledged."

Aaron's mom sees it differently:

"I knew that my son was going to be exposed to Christmas, and I'm fine with that. What I object to is that Christmas is the only theme for the whole month of December! One day for Hanukah and thirty days for Christmas. Aaron is getting inundated with it. It's not just the commercial side of the holiday. She is reading stories about Jesus and has him singing religious carols. Now he wants to know why we can't have Christmas. She has Santa Claus coming to the house this week. I don't know what to do."

What Is the Problem?

The issue surrounding holidays tends to be either about religious or cultural diversity or about commercialism. The diversity side of the issue involves supporting families' beliefs and values. While spending a day (or week) on each holiday seems fair to you, it is important to hear that it doesn't feel fair to the family who is not a part of majority American culture. If the experiences of your family do not match what is on television, in newspapers and magazines, and on display on every street corner, it is hard for families to enculturate their children. All American children, regardless of their religion or culture, become experts on Christmas, Easter, Halloween, and Thanksgiving. If children are raised in families that celebrate these holidays, it is easy to be completely ignorant about other holidays and beliefs.

Holidays are especially tough for families who believe it is wrong to celebrate them. Some fundamentalist Christian families do not want their children exposed to Halloween, which is considered a pagan holiday. Jehovah's Witnesses may not celebrate any holidays or birthdays.

The other issue that comes up is the focus on commercialism. Even families who celebrate holidays may object to the focus on Madison Avenue and the "gimme" aspect of holidays. While these families might be pleased with a focus on family traditions, Santa Claus, the Easter Bunny, and other nonreligious traditions might undermine family values.

What Are You Thinking?

Be aware of how your reaction might make the situation worse. It is easier to move into finding positive solutions if you can avoid getting into the following mind-sets, recognizing them as unhelpful to developing a healthy partnership with parents. Typical defensive reactions include these:

☀ *"The parent is telling me what to do in my own classroom (or home or program)."*
It can make you angry if you feel like you are being bullied in your own environment. If you can push past this feeling to think about the immediate issue, the emotions won't run the show.

☀ *"The desires of the most demanding parents will overwhelm the rest."*
This can feel almost undemocratic. Resist resorting to majority rule, and find a solution that everyone can live with.

☀ *"If the religious aspects of a holiday aren't allowed, we are trivializing something important and perpetuating commercialism."*
This again comes down to values. Focus on what really matters to you rather than creating a compromise that is dissatisfying to everyone involved, such as not including any of the holiday's religious parts.

What Are Parents Thinking?

Thinking about how our actions strike emotional chords with parents (just as theirs do with us) can help us to be more sensitive.

☀ *"The teacher thinks her values are more important than mine."*
This is especially challenging if your culture or religion has been marginalized in the past.

Solving the Problem

Once a family objects to your focus on a holiday, you need to decide what you are willing to compromise.

☀ *Listen to the parent's feelings.*
This may be the most important step if this parent perceives that she hasn't been listened to before on this matter. Reflect back her feelings so she knows you truly heard her.

⚙ *Share your feelings.*
Don't let your feelings get personal. These are emotional issues, and you can be firm without belittling different beliefs or traditions. "I understand this has made you uncomfortable. I didn't think about that. Christmas is such a joyous time in our family I just wanted to share it with the children."

⚙ *Find a compromise.*
Approach the family in a nondefensive manner, and figure out what you can both live with. Are there days the family is planning to be away? If so, this is a good time to concentrate on the activities they have the least comfort with. Maybe you can allow the family to take absence on those days without charging them. I taught a child whose mother had died the previous year. I met with his guardians, who had talked to a psychologist, to make a plan to reduce the trauma of Mother's Day. We decided to save some stories and other activities for days he would be absent, hoping he would not be as tender next year.

After the Problem Is Solved: Moving Toward True Partnership

⚙ *Create a plan with families.*
Involve parents in a focused discussion about celebrations so you won't be surprised by their reactions. You can talk as a group—parents and staff—about shared values over traditions and celebrations. The group can write a "position statement" or some document that details what they want children to learn about their own family traditions, the beliefs and traditions of others, and common values and experiences. You can then refer to this document when making future holiday plans. While this may feel like giving up a lot of control, you are building support for your curriculum.

⚙ *Create new celebrations for your program.*
You can enjoy all of the festivities of holidays without stepping on anyone's toes. Maybe you have major celebrations over losing a tooth or the birthday of a favorite author. For more suggestions about new school traditions, read Bonnie Neugebauer's article "Going One Step Further—No Traditional Holidays" (1994).

Before You Have Problems

Read through the following list and check off what you have already accomplished (see pages 72–75). If many of the checkboxes are blank, you have work to do to create an environment where problems are easy to solve.

☐ *Focus on developing common ground.*
Acknowledge to yourself that you cannot develop a values-free curriculum. Explain what you will celebrate and why.

☐ *Develop shared understanding as new families enter your program.*
Make sure materials that go to prospective families have enough information to evaluate if the program is a good match with their values. When a child enters your program, be sure families understand your curriculum. Be as specific as possible about activities, plans, and alternatives. Put it in writing. Make sure there is a section in your parent handbook about holiday policies.

☐ *Focus on the connection between program goals and curriculum decisions.*
Make sure parents are prepared for each new event. Remind them ahead of time. Send out a note a month before a holiday explaining what you will do and why, and what you want from parents. If your program begins in the fall, Halloween tends to be the first big holiday to face. If you don't want masks, costumes, or candy, tell parents clearly and tell them why. Some examples: Masks are too scary for younger or sensitive children; costumes may tear and disappoint children or make children too excitable; you avoid sweets in your program and know children will already be getting a lot of candy elsewhere; you have so many interesting things to focus on in your program, and you don't think Halloween is worth the attention. Even if you have told them before, they may have not processed what it means. "You mean my daughter can't even wear her costume? We weren't planning on trick-or-treating so I only bought it for school."

. . . .

Scenario 2: Controlling Pretend Play, or, "Not my son!"

Monique feels challenged by this father's attitude:

> "We offer a developmentally ap-
> propriate program here, and part
> of that includes supporting chil-
> dren's sociodramatic play. I find
> the children who spend a lot of
> time in the housekeeping corner
> to be the ones who need that
> play the most. Logan is a sweet
> little boy who loves to dress up.
> He comes in every day, puts on
> the same Cinderella-type gown,
> and then joins classroom activi-
> ties. His mom is fine with it, but
> his dad is clearly uncomfortable.
> He makes fun of Logan and tells
> him he's acting like a sissy. We
> had our parent-teacher confer-
> ence last week, and his dad told
> me he doesn't want me to let
> Logan dress up in girls' clothing
> anymore. I don't know what to
> do."

Larry is concerned:

> "It's not like I'm afraid my son is
> gay, but I don't like it when he
> dresses up like a girl. This is the
> age when children are learning
> values. If we don't teach him
> what it means to be male, he
> might be confused. The teacher
> and my wife don't understand
> how tough it is to grow up male.
> Kids are not going to understand
> if he wants to wear dresses in
> kindergarten! I don't want my
> son to be teased or get beat up
> because he doesn't know how to
> be a boy. I am just trying to act
> now to avoid problems in the
> future."

What Is the Problem?

Parents are naturally concerned that they will lose influence over their children when other adults play such a significant role in their lives. Parents do
not want to make a mistake that will have a negative impact on their children. Some parents are surprised to find out how conservative their values
are once they are raising children.

What Are You Thinking?

Be aware of how your reaction might make the situation worse. It is easier
to move into finding positive solutions if you can avoid getting into the following mind-sets, recognizing them as unhelpful to developing a healthy
partnership with parents. Typical defensive reactions include these:

☀ *"This parent is trying to impose his prejudices onto the classroom."*
Creating a values-free classroom isn't possible. Every choice you make, from the way you arrange the physical environment to the books you read and the hours you are open, reflects your values. When families are in agreement with these values they become almost invisible. When families differ in opinion, values stick out and can be the source of conflict.

☀ *"If I take dress up out of my classroom, then I have rewarded the squeaky wheel."*
You assume that families have chosen your program due, in some part, to common values. You don't want to give up something that is important to you and to the other families. Rather than thinking of this as a power struggle with a winner and a loser, think of it as a highly emotional issue that requires careful consideration.

What Are Parents Thinking?

Thinking about how our actions strike emotional chords with parents (just as theirs do with us) can help us to be more sensitive.

☀ *"The teachers don't understand how this can affect my child."*
Culture has a strong influence over gender expectations. Families are expected to prepare their children to be functioning members of their culture. When those cultural expectations are at odds with the culture of the school, it creates conflict. If it is important to you to have a multi-cultural program, you will need to come to terms with these issues.

Solving the Problem

☀ *Hear the families' concerns.*
Families may have information about their lives that you are not aware of. Even if you don't agree in the end, it will help you develop a relationship.

☀ *Explain why you think the activity is important for their child.*
Help families to see behavior within the context of the child's current developmental stage. We know that most little boys who like to play dress up don't grow up to be gay or transvestites, but parents don't have the breadth of experience we do. They may need reassuring. Remind parents that the fun of Halloween costumes is wearing what you would not otherwise wear.

☀ *Suggest a limited risk.*
Ask parents to give the child time to lose interest in the play. Most children that play constantly with one game or activity eventually finish and move on.

☀ *Find a supportive third person for the family.*
Ask the parent of an older child who went through a stage of dressing up and moved on to talk to this family. Getting permission from both families before mentioning each to the other is tricky, but it can be a valuable experience.

☀ *Work with the family to find common goals for the child.*
Most parents would not be attracted to our programs if they did not see some common ground. An example of seemingly opposite family preferences attracted to the same program is a preschool on a nature center, which attracted both parents who were hunters and parents who were vegetarians. Both were interested in a program that included a nature component. A comfort level was found when differences were shared and home values were supported, and children had lively discussions on the topic. The same can happen in programs with children from different religions. The most important value to reinforce is "That's what you do in your family."

After the Problem Is Solved: Move Toward True Partnership

Rather than providing prepared costumes, some programs give children the materials to make their own dress-up outfits. Pieces of fabric, paper, scissors, tape, beads for making jewelry, and similar materials can bring out more creativity in children.

Before You Have Problems

Read through the following list and check off what you have already accomplished (see pages 72–75). If many of the checkboxes are blank, you have work to do to create an environment where problems are easy to solve.

☐ *Focus on developing common ground.*
Acknowledge to yourself that you cannot develop a values-free curriculum. Put the program's goals and values in writing. This can be done in a brochure, on a Web site, or in another format. Being as open as possible helps parents know if this program is a good fit for their family. If families know that creative self-expression and fantasy play are an important part of your program, they may be better prepared.

☐ *Develop shared understanding as new families enter your program.*
Make sure materials that go to prospective families have enough information to evaluate if the program is a good match with their values. Give clear information about classroom activities before families enroll.

Offering families tours of the school during free playtime will help them see typical activities. Give them a chance to ask questions after the tour.

☐ *Focus on the connection between program goals and curriculum decisions.*
Help parents see the connection between program goals and children's development. The connection between pretend play and development is not as clear to parents as it is to us. Take time during parent-teacher conferences, parent meetings, newsletters, and other forms of communication to connect the dots for families.

☐ *Practice flexibility.*
Make sure you have attractive dress-up clothes that boys would wear, as well as dress-up clothes for girls. If a child senses that his parents don't like him dressing up in girls' clothes, he is stuck either complying with their demands or feeling guilty when he does not. You can save him from this conflict by providing items that are glitzy and fancy and that lend themselves to fantasy play without being clearly for females. Some examples include the sequined vests of bullfighters, little tuxedo jackets, sports clothing, animal costumes, and kings' robes and crowns. Or, create a dress-up collection that isn't gender specific. Robes, occupational costumes, and animal costumes will be less likely to make parents uncomfortable.

Scenario 3: Fear of Losing Influence over One's Own Child, or, "Whose child is this, anyway?"

Tamara is annoyed:

"When the Smiths enrolled their daughter, Paige, in my program, they told me that they didn't have a television in their home and didn't want her watching TV. We agreed that if the other children were watching a video, I would give her an art activity in the kitchen. Paige's parents made it sound as if she would go along with it. Well, she won't. She feels left out when the other children are watching TV and she is made to stay out of the room. It makes me feel guilty for having the television on. I find myself trying to talk the kids out of a video. Before Paige came, we had a nice routine of the older children having quiet time in front of a video while the little kids were napping. Now I find myself turning the whole house upside down to satisfy the parents' demands. Even though I don't let her watch the videos, her parents complain that she is picking up TV stuff, and they don't like it."

Mrs. Smith feels tricked:

"Raising our children according to our values is important to us. We don't like what television does to children. It makes them more violent and less compassionate. It also encourages commercialism. When we enrolled Paige in the family child care program we noticed there was a TV, and we shared our concerns. Tamara told us the kids hardly ever watch TV and agreed to provide an alternative activity for Paige if the television was on. Well, 'hardly ever' turns out to mean every day! It's obvious that Tamara resents having to come up with a different activity for Paige so she just throws playdough on a table in the kitchen. She says Paige doesn't want to stay in the kitchen—who can blame her? We don't see why she can't just come up with something more positive than plopping the children in front of the TV. Tamara says she doesn't let Paige watch it, but Paige is coming home singing cartoon theme songs and whining for toys we have never told her about. She must be getting that from TV."

What Is the Problem?

This issue is twofold. First, the parents have a different vision of what family child care should look like than the caregiver has. Second, they are concerned that they are losing control over their child's values.

Parents who choose to place their children in family child care may have different versions of what they hope their children will experience. For some, it is an experience close to what they would have if they stayed home. These parents may appreciate the homelike touches of children eating at a kitchen table (rather than a classroom table), playing in a living room or backyard, playing with children in a variety of ages as would be experienced in an extended family, and having a relaxed atmosphere that is more like home than an institutional school. For families with this vision, it may seem normal for children to watch television on occasion as they might at home, or they might expect that TV would be avoided because of the smaller group size and more relaxed atmosphere. Others may be viewing family child care as preschool on a smaller scale. They may expect a more school-like atmosphere with more rigid schedules, structured activities, and "learning" as the primary goal of all activities during the day. For these parents, TV may seem inappropriate.

Further, some parents feel at constant war with media and other institutions for controlling their children's values. They may resent the push for commercialism. They may dislike the exposure to violence, sex, or other themes they believe to be at odds with their own convictions. They may want to choose when to broach certain topics with their children rather than having their children receive information (or misinformation) from others.

What Are You Thinking?

Be aware of how your reaction might make the situation worse. It is easier to move into finding positive solutions if you can avoid getting into the following mind-sets, recognizing them as unhelpful to developing a healthy partnership with parents. Typical defensive reactions include these:

☀ *"This parent doesn't think I am doing a good job."*
It is hard to not feel judged by parental criticism. Letting go of your defensiveness and listening to parental concerns is more productive.

☀ *"The parent is trying to control what goes on in my house."*
When you open your house up to family child care, you turn your home into a business. You give up some of the privacy and control you had before.

☀ *"The parent is going to insist on changes that ruin everything that is working so well!"*
When a program is running smoothly, contemplating change becomes hard. Try to open up to truly considering making changes so that your own fear of change doesn't keep you from evaluating the situation.

What Are Parents Thinking?

Thinking about how our actions strike emotional chords with parents (just as theirs do with us) can help us to be more sensitive.

☀ *"The caregiver doesn't care what we want."*
"She is just going to do whatever is easiest for her, not what's right for my child." It's a powerless feeling to be unable to control the influence on your child.

☀ *"I don't want my child exposed to this influence!"*
Are there religious issues for the families in your program? Some fundamentalist religions are especially concerned with the influence of television.

Solving the Problem

Once you discover that the parent's expectations do not match your plans, provide information to help everyone decide if this is the best placement.

☀ *Avoid getting defensive.*
The disagreement isn't about you, it's about their child.

☀ *Remember, the parents' role is as advocate for their child and family.*
Don't expect them to care about what the other parents or children want. Their focus is their own child. Your job is to watch out for the interests of the other families.

☀ *Make a plan with the parents that you can both live with.*
Put the plan in writing so both groups leave with the same version. Agree to revisit the issue at a later date.

After the Problem Is Solved: Move Toward True Partnership

☀ *Invite the parents to send ideas.*
Have the parents suggest projects that would serve the same goal as watching TV, a quiet, restful activity for the children. Books on tape might be a good alternative.

☀ *Research professional journals.*
Research the effects of TV watching for children and recommendations from the field. The National Association for the Education of Young Children (NAEYC) has a position statement on passive media use.

☀ *Conduct a parent survey.*
See how the other parents in your program feel about the use of TV. More families than you know may be concerned.

Before You Have Problems

Read through the following list and check off what you have already accomplished (see pages 72–75). If many of the checkboxes are blank, you have work to do to create an environment where problems are easy to solve.

☐ *Develop shared understanding as new families enter your program.*
Make sure materials that go to perspective families have enough information to evaluate if the program is a good match with their values. Give accurate information about your program before a family enrolls. Don't use terms like *occasionally* or *hardly ever* as they may mean "once per week" to you and "once per year" to the parents. Provide a clear picture of what a typical day looks like as well as the less-typical day. What do you do if it's raining? What do you do if one of your children is sick and separated in his bedroom? How do you treat special occasions? Be clear about your rules. Can children bring in videos to share? Which videos? Do you stay in the room with children who are watching television? Which network shows can children watch?

☐ *Focus on the connection between program goals and curriculum decisions.*
Be clear about your program's goals. You cannot be all things to all people. You have a limited number of families you can serve. Everyone will have a better experience if you are on the same page about what children are going to experience.

☐ *Spend time with families to learn about their values.*
Understand parents' expectations. Do they expect you to offer a unique activity for their child? Do they hope you will discourage watching television? How hard do they expect you to work to keep their child from catching a glimpse of TV? Do they expect you to limit pretend play that involves TV characters?

Discussion Questions

1. When you were growing up, was your family very much like the families of your schoolmates? How accepting were classmates and teachers of different families?
2. What values and beliefs are most central to your work with children? How are those reflected in your practices and policies?
3. If you currently work with children, how much diversity is there among your families? How have you accommodated their values and beliefs?

☀ 4 ☀

Child Development Issues

While various philosophies influence early childhood programs, child development has a shared knowledge base. Parents don't have that luxury. While teachers can refer to research, parents are getting advice from in-laws, friends, and the latest articles in the press. What may seem clear to us may seem like a fad to parents. Spank or don't spank? Pacifiers? Academics or play-based programs? We can change our minds about our style of teaching, but parents must live with the consequences of their mistakes. If we keep in mind the conflicting information and high stakes parents must contend with, it is easier to be patient when we disagree.

Talking to Parents about Stages of Development

One of the gifts we offer parents is information about typical child development. While parents know more than teachers about their own children, we have the broad knowledge that comes from spending time with many children of the same age. In addition, teachers have information about child development research from classes, reading, and professional development. Some conflicts between parents and teachers come from this difference in confidence about what is true in child development. While listening to what parents know about their children is important, we can also alleviate concerns by sharing information with parents about stages of child development. Some of these issues include discipline, academics versus play-based programs, toilet training, and biting, lying, and other age-specific behaviors.

❄ **Discipline.**

Teachers tend to have clear ideas about what kind of discipline is appropriate for young children, and it is one of the areas we are quickest to judge parents about. The most common complaint that teachers have about parents is lack of consistency. We need to remember that it is much easier to be consistent in school than it is at home. We have an environment that is exclusively (or almost exclusively) used for young children. We don't have dangerous or fragile objects around as most homes do. We aren't trying to get other things done (such as cleaning or working) at the same time we are with children. We are fresh (at least compared to parents who may have just woken up, worked a ten-hour shift, or driven a long commute). At our best we are doing something we were trained to do, and we are not personally embarrassed by the behavior of the children.

Before I was a mother, I would watch a child crying in a shopping cart and think, "What is that horrible parent doing to that poor child?" After I joined the parenthood club, I would react by thinking, "That poor mom!" Before you become frustrated with the parent who reacts instead of taking positive action, gives in to whining children, or behaves in an inconsistent manner, think about how much more challenging it is to parent for life than it is to teach for eight or fewer hours per day.

❄ **Academics vs. play-based programs.**

Teachers have the support of organizations, such as the National Association for the Education of Young Children (NAEYC), to inform our opinions on what kind of education is best for young children. Parents are judged by everyone. They have the memories of their own schooling (and most people cannot remember their own preschool experiences so they are really thinking back to first grade) and assume that what was exciting, scary, or difficult for them will seem that way to their children. Grandparents and other relatives are more than happy to share opinions. For every article about the Hurried Child there is another telling them not to let their children be left behind. Knowing this, you shouldn't be surprised if parents aren't quick to trust that you know what form of education is best for their children.

❄ **Toilet training.**

Teachers have accepted practices that support children's toilet learning. Even our practices have changed a little recently as pediatricians are now saying later is better for many children. Parents have much less experience in toilet training than we do (how many children does the average toddler teacher toilet train in her career?), less ideal circumstances to do it (we don't have children in restaurants, on vacation, in a snowsuit, or on the way to the grocery store), and less trust that it will all happen. We might say, "I've never sent a child off to college in diapers," but the parent is worried about kindergarten. Even our policies tend to send mixed messages to parents. Many preschool programs won't take children who are not toilet trained, and then we judge parents for trying to rush children out of diapers! If we understand why toilet training is so hard for parents, we can work more closely with them when their children are at this stage and be more understanding when they are less than consistent.

❊ **Biting, lying, and other age-specific behaviors.**
Teachers have seen trends in behaviors that are related to development. Children who do not have the language skills to communicate when frustrated are more likely to bite than older, more competent children. We don't worry that toddlers who bite will grow up to be ax murderers, but parents don't have the experience of watching many children outgrow this behavior or the distance to not take it personally. When young children do not tell the truth, we understand that fantasy versus reality is not fixed for them. Parents are thinking about their children's character and are understandably on the watch for flaws while they still can take action to correct personality traits that will have a negative effect on their children's lives. If we understand how loaded these issues are for parents, we can give them good information about child development so they can view these behaviors with less concern.

Support Parents' Understanding of Their Children's Development

The first step is creating fair policies that support the mission and goals of the program by keeping a few key things in mind:

1. Keep in mind that development is dynamic.
2. Offer parents information about development and resources for learning more.
3. Share information with parents about child guidance.
4. Remember that there is more than one right way to work with children.
5. Support parents' choices.

Keep in mind that development is dynamic. As a field, we have moved beyond the lockstep notions of what two-year-olds are like or what three-year-olds are like that were established in the 1920s. We now understand that innate qualities, family life, culture, experience, and other factors all affect development. We will serve children and families better if we don't expect all children of the same chronological age to be on the same page. We can help parents focus on children developing greater competency (such as learning to comfort themselves, tying shoes, or reading their names) rather than giving them the message that a child should already be doing those things.

Offer parents information about development and resources for learning more. For many families, we are the primary avenue for parent education. By taking this responsibility seriously and making information accessible, we will help parents be their most competent. The side benefit for us is that parents who are more informed can support what we are doing in the classroom. We can share information formally by offering lending libraries, child development information in parent newsletters, lectures on parenting, ideas for home activities, a toy lending library, comprehensive parent-teacher conferences, and announcing public programs for parents. Many parents find the most beneficial methods to be casual conversations about what their children are doing and how that fits in the greater scheme of development. Another great avenue for teaching parents about development is by displaying their children's classroom work with explanatory messages.

Share information with parents about child guidance. Many parents find discipline challenging at one time or another. Most parents really appreciate having teachers they can talk to about struggles at home including eating, sleeping, sibling rivalry, and other situations that don't come up at school. Rather than frame advice as "You should . . . ," you can make suggestions such as, "Some parents have been successful by . . ."

Remember that there is more than one correct way to work with children. While it helps parents when we provide information about child guidance, teachers can step over the line into prescribing solutions that don't fit the families. In the end, parents need to make their own choices. You may be uncomfortable with methods such as bribery, but it may fit the culture of the family.

Support the choices parents make. Parents need our support. If they don't want children eating certain foods, we need to support them even if we think it is silly. They don't need us judging their decisions. Most of us have plenty of relatives to do that for us!

When Nothing Seems to Work

Dealing with the learning curve some parents have when learning about child development is frustrating. Many teachers want parents to agree with their positions, accept their knowledge and opinions unconditionally, or want the families out of the program. If we don't accept that parents have something to teach us and that they will sometimes be right (does that make us wrong?), we will be missing great learning opportunities for ourselves. Even if differences in opinion are based on parents' misunderstandings about typical child development, we shouldn't give up on them too fast. By helping parents become more competent, we will have an effect on children that lasts long beyond their years with us.

If you are considering asking a parent to find another program, ask yourself the following questions:

※ Do the parents' actions in response to their child's development interfere with the safety and well-being of other children in the program?
※ Even if this is true, is the child's behavior showing improvement?
※ Can you maintain a positive relationship with the family even if they aren't on the same page with you on this issue?

The following are more detailed examples of issues related to child development.

Scenarios

• •

Scenario 1: Taking School Toys Home, or, "My little Jesse James."

Joe doesn't understand why the parent got so agitated:

> "I noticed some of our Matchbox cars were disappearing when I prepared the classroom before school each day. I started watching and, sure enough, Marty was slipping toy cars into his pocket during clean-up time. My co-teacher and I had a chuckle. She talked to Marty's mom about it, and she agreed to check his pants when he got home. As he was leaving on Tuesday I noticed a bulge in his pants' pocket so I stopped him and checked. I found a car and reminded him gently about leaving school toys at school. It was no big deal. That evening, his mom called my coteacher at home and said I had humiliated her. She wanted me to apologize! I didn't accuse her of stealing!"

Marty's mom is seething:

> "I was so embarrassed! Marty's teacher called him a thief right in front of all the other families! Marty is a little forgetful and probably just put the car in his pocket during clean up and forgot it was there. Joe seems to have it out for him. He searched his pockets, right there in front of everyone. I can't even talk to Joe anymore."

What Is the Problem?

Two issues cloud this scenario: parents' lack of insight into developmental understanding of ownership and the way feedback about a child can feel personal to a parent.

One of the best pieces written on developmental understanding of ownership is called, "Toddler's Rules of Possession." (It appears, unattributed, on many Web sites. Just search for the title on the Web and you'll be able to read the whole list.) The author does an amusing job of portraying the wishful thinking ("If I saw it first, it's mine") of young children. As educators, we have vast experience with this thinking and don't view such action as thievery. Parents are less likely to understand this, and any "borrowing" of toys can make a parent worry that they have a budding kleptomaniac on their hands.

The second issue of personalization also complicates this scenario. Parents identify so closely with their children that they can experience criticism of their child as criticism of themselves.

What Are You Thinking?

Be aware of how your reaction might make the situation worse. It is easier to move into finding positive solutions if you can avoid getting into the following mind-sets, recognizing them as unhelpful to developing a healthy partnership with parents. Typical defensive reactions include these:

※ *"This mom is deflecting her embarrassment by finding fault with my behavior!"*
This may be true, but it is human nature. If you can avoid embarrassing people, they don't have to defend themselves by attacking you.

※ *"The mother is putting words in my mouth! I didn't say her son was a thief."*
This can be frustrating, but if you understand how parents hear your words, it will be easier to clear up the disagreement.

※ *"The mother is enabling her son by focusing on what I did and not what he did."*
A parent will naturally try to protect her child. Finding a way to express concerns delicately can avoid defensiveness.

※ *"She just blew this all out of proportion. Before this Marty and I had a great relationship, and now he thinks I don't like him."*
Try not to allow the problem between the adults to change your relationship to the child.

What Are Parents Thinking?

Thinking about how our actions strike emotional chords with parents (just as theirs do with us) can help us to be more sensitive.

※ *"The teacher accused my child of stealing!"*
You never know what experiences parents bring to adulthood. If parents have been unjustly accused of a misdeed in their own childhood, they are likely to meet a similar issue involving their children defensively.

※ *"What's the big deal? It's just a cheap car!"*
Different cultures have different attitudes about ownership. A parent may think that you have plenty of cars. It won't be a problem for her child to take one.

❋ *"Joe doesn't trust me to handle this."*
From the perspective of the parent, Joe asked her to deal with an issue and then didn't give her a chance to do so. From Joe's perspective, he was helping and supporting the parent by following through.

Solving the Problem

Getting back into a trusting relationship with this parent will take some work.

❋ *Hear how the parent feels.*
Rather than starting to defend yourself, really listen to the parent talk about both what they think and what they feel. Use a reflective message to let her know you understand: "So you were planning on checking for toys when you had more privacy. When I brought it up in front of other families, it was embarrassing for you."

❋ *Explain why you did what you did.*
"I didn't realize it would feel that way to you. I thought if I was matter-of-fact about the whole thing, it wouldn't be a big deal."

❋ *Make sure the parent knows you have positive feelings for her child.*
"I know Marty didn't mean to steal it. At this age, children still think that wishing something were theirs has the power to make it so. I admire that Marty knows what he wants!"

❋ *Help the parent understand that the behavior is normal.*
Refer parents to a book such as *Practical Solutions for Practically Every Problem* (Saifer 2003) to help put the issue in perspective.

❋ *Assure the parent that you will be more sensitive to confidentiality in the future.*
Parents have the right to privacy about potential misdeeds of their children.

After the Problem Is Solved: Moving Toward True Partnership

❋ *Let children borrow books and toys from school.*
Allowing families to borrow toys and books helps keep possessions to a minimum (a child only needs to work with the same puzzle so many times) and is a great way to experience sharing.

Before You Have Problems

Read through the following list and check off what you have already accomplished (see pages 89–93). If many of the checkboxes are blank, you have work to do to create an environment where problems are easy to solve.

☐ *Offer parents information about development and resources for learning more.*
Your parent library can be full of books on development issues. Copy a page on issues common to this age group, such as "taking what isn't yours," and post it on your parent bulletin board or in class newsletters.

☐ *Share information with parents about child guidance.*
Model examining issues from the child's perspective. If parents see us asking questions to learn why children behave in certain ways (maybe the child has a toy just like it at home) then they will not feel as judged or embarrassed when an issue comes up.

● ●

Scenario 2: The Parent Who Personalizes Her Child's Rejection, or, "Then you can't come to my birthday party."

Pam describes her frustration:

"Four-year-olds are experimenting with friendship. They proclaim best friends, get in fights, hate each other, and are best friends again before lunch. It is no big deal until the parents get involved. Olivia's mom takes it so seriously. She heard that one of the other children was having a party and didn't invite Olivia. She showed up in tears and didn't want me to let the children talk about it at school. She called the parents of the other little girls and cried about how much Olivia was devastated by the whole thing. Olivia doesn't seem devastated. She still plays with the other child. The mom of the birthday girl came to me so embarrassed. She doesn't want to have all of the kids over for a party, and I think that is her right. But the bad feelings are taking over the whole school. Parents are talking in the parking lot. I don't know what to do!"

Olivia's mom explains how she feels:

"It's just so hurtful. Olivia just loves this little girl, Beth. Beth is one of those power-hungry little girls who acts like the queen of the class. She is having this big party and never misses an opportunity to point out to Olivia that she isn't coming. I could just slap Beth's smug little face. I tried appealing to her mother about how important this is for Olivia, but she is just like her daughter. Her teacher doesn't understand how hard this is on Olivia. If they are all so unfeeling, maybe she'd be better off in another school."

What Is the Problem?

Parents bring to the classroom all of their own history and baggage. It is not unusual for this to show up when parents react to a rejection or other negative experience as if it happened to them instead. Expecting a parent to be logical will not help you. Appealing to a parent's sense of proportion is also unlikely to be successful. If you do not acknowledge the parent's feelings and help them move on, you are likely to encounter this issue again.

What Are You Thinking?

Be aware of how your reaction might make the situation worse. It is easier to move into finding positive solutions if you can avoid getting into the following mind-sets, recognizing them as unhelpful to developing a healthy partnership with parents. Typical defensive reactions include these:

☀ *"This parent is crazy."*
It is reasonable to be cautious about your involvement with unbalanced parents, but it's more helpful to begin with the assumption that this is a blind spot in an otherwise normal person.

☀ *"I am getting dragged into issues that are not in my job description."*
Your first focus should be on the children, and it is important that you do not allow the drama of the adults to become your focus. It is also true that the emotions of parents follow their children into the school. If you ignore them, you lose the opportunity to keep them from getting out of control.

☀ *"This parent is turning her child into a princess."*
It is difficult to watch a parent miss an opportunity to teach her child resiliency. You cannot change a parent's basic beliefs but you can model other ways of interaction.

What Are Parents Thinking?

Thinking about how our actions strike emotional chords with parents (just as theirs do with us) can help us to be more sensitive.

☀ *"This school teaches children to be self-centered."*
In some cultures, the good of the whole group takes precedence over the good of the individual. I had a Japanese parent confront me on my ethnocentric policies that placed priority on the individual's right to choose playmates over the well-being of the whole class when such exclusion was allowed. It made an impact on me because it was her child that was doing the excluding, and she didn't want me to allow him to do so.

☀ *"This is an insult to all of us."*
Saving face for the family is an issue in some cultures, and a slight to the child is a slight to the whole family. In many cultures, an egocentric parent isn't the only one that takes such actions personally. It is a basis for community harmony. If this is the case, you can take the role of "cultural translator" and help the other parent see why this is an issue.

☀ *"I have failed my daughter. I have not taught her to make friends."*
If the parent's cultural identity is largely set by her role as a mother, it will be harder for her to separate herself from her child. I mentored an international program in which nonworking mothers in foreign countries were placed in the difficult position where their husband's corporate expectation was to place the children in a full-day program. These mothers were torn between needing to support their husband's career by placing their children with the other expatriate children and their need to be with their children in this place where they knew nobody. The program wisely created many activities and reasons for mothers to spend a large part of the day helping in the library, office, and other parts of the program without interfering with their children's adjustment to school.

Solving the Problem

Once the problem has started, you can take the teachable moment to help the parent differentiate between herself and her child.

☀ *Hear and reflect your understanding of the parent's pain.*
Reassure the parent that you will be sensitive to emotional undercurrents at school. "It must be so hard to think that your child is getting rejected. I don't want children to have that experience, and I keep an eye on how children treat each other at school."

☀ *Help the parent understand the typical social world of children of this age.*
"What I have seen is that at this age, children are best friends on the playground, mad at each other during snack, and forget all about it by nap."

☀ *Suggest to the mom that she try to stay neutral.*
Staying neutral makes it easier for friendships to mend when this event has been forgotten. "If you resist giving it attention, it will be easier for Olivia to regain her friendship with Beth."

☀ *Help parents see this as an opportunity to develop resilience in their children.*
"If Olivia can learn to ignore children when they behave this way, she will inoculate herself against peer pressure." While watching this process, Olivia's mom may become more resilient herself.

☀ *Avoid getting dragged into the dispute.*
Be very careful not to take sides with one parent or to say or do anything that can be viewed as taking sides. When one is in conflict with another person, garnering allies is natural. Refuse to say anything about the other

parent, even if you have information that might help the other parent understand the situation better. For example, it's not your place to say, "She has a small house and couldn't fit more children in it for a party."

☀ *Offer stories to help parents develop perspective.*
Using examples of your own experiences to illustrate a point can be helpful. "I remember when my son was that age, another child said something mean to him and it upset me so much, I didn't even want to see the mom. The children were over it in a few days. My job was to put my feelings aside and be happy for my son's closure on the whole thing."

☀ *Don't let the dispute follow the families into the program.*
Pretend you don't know anything about it. Don't arrange for the families to stay away from each other in school or make other allowances for the event.

☀ *Don't allow adults to make negative statements about other families or children in your presence.*
If you see a cluster of parents gossiping, nicely but firmly ask them to take it outdoors.

After the Problem Is Solved: Moving Toward True Partnership

☀ *Help parents connect.*
Part of creating a sense of community within the classroom includes creating a sense of community with the families. If parents come to know each other well in the context of school, behavior that might hurt feelings will be less likely to take place. Classroom involvement, PTA-type organizations, and parent education classes are all opportunities for families to get to know each other.

☀ *Offer parenting classes.*
Parenting classes can offer adults the chance to deal with their own issues that come up within the context of parenting. A parenting class in our Minnesota community had parents read Vivian Paley's *You Can't Say You Can't Play* (1992), which deals with exclusion and ways to create a rejection-free zone in your classroom. Parents who read this book dealt with their own experiences growing up and were able to differentiate between their experiences and those of their children with greater ease.

Before You Have Problems

Read through the following list and check off what you have already accomplished (see pages 89–93). If many of the checkboxes are blank, you have work to do to create an environment where problems are easy to solve.

☐ *Offer parents information about development and resources for learning more.*
Parents may not think about the ramifications of including some classmates and excluding others. Set the parameters for the intersections between family and school life. In this particular case, steps could have been taken to not allow invitations to be passed out at school. Olivia's mom could use information about friendship patterns for children at this age.

☐ *Share information with parents about child guidance.*
Give parents guidance in beginning their children's social lives outside of school. One common rule of thumb is one invitee for each year the child has achieved. This would mean that a three-year-old would invite only three friends.

☐ *Support parents' choices.*
You can help parents stay out of this predicament by providing celebrations at school. While some schools do not want social events to take over the program, this can be especially appropriate in family child care settings.

• •

Scenario 3: The New School Year, or, "Where are my daughter's friends?"

Shannon feels hassled by this parent's complaints:

"We put a lot of time and energy into placing children in classes for the new school year. The teachers for the two-year-old rooms help us divide up the kids who are going to the three-year-old rooms. We told Tanya's mother she was going to be in my class this year, and she seemed happy about it. Now it's the third day of school and she wants Tanya moved to the other class for threes. She says all of Tanya's friends are in there and Tanya doesn't want to come to school anymore. Mom thinks it's a problem that we didn't put Tanya in the same class as her friend Erica. We intentionally placed them in different classes. We want Tanya to show more independence—she did everything Erica told her to. Why can't Tanya's mom understand this is for her own good?"

Tanya's mom is surprised by her daughter's tears:

"I wasn't prepared for Tanya to have such a hard time settling into school this year. Last year we knew it would be tough. She was only two, and we spent a long time helping her through the transition. Now she knows this school and the routines and seemed like she was really happy to come to the big class. We didn't realize none of her friends would be with her. I can't take another year of her crying about school. If they would just move her, I know it would be okay."

What Is the Problem?

Watching their child go from loving school to not wanting to go can be devastating for parents. Parents often ask children why they don't like school, and most children don't have the ability to verbalize their gut feelings. They try to express their unhappiness and parents leap to fix the problem. Teachers have the experience to know that a resistant child will likely settle in if the program has been successful for the child in the past. They want parents to show patience in the adjustment process. Parents are focused on wanting their child to be happy.

What Are You Thinking?

Be aware of how your reaction might make the situation worse. It is easier to move into finding positive solutions if you can avoid getting into the following mind-sets, recognizing them as unhelpful to developing a healthy partnership with parents. Typical defensive reactions include these:

❋ *"This parent is asking to pull her child out of my class! Doesn't she think I'm a good teacher?"*
It's easy to take this personally, but the parent is focused on what she can do to make her child come to school willingly. If you become defensive, it will damage your relationship with this family.

❋ *"Doesn't this mom have any confidence in her daughter's ability to make new friends?"*
It is not uncommon for parents to be insecure about their child's social abilities. This can be especially true if the parent had issues in this area growing up. She isn't going to be convinced otherwise by your words. She needs to experience her child's social competence.

❋ *"This mom wants us all to jump through hoops to give her daughter her way. How are we supposed to make room in that class for another child?"*
Remember, the parent is not focused on what is fair for other children, she is trying to advocate for her own child's needs. You will get farther by helping parents see how sticking with a placement will benefit their child rather than by appealing to their sense of fair play.

What Are Parents Thinking?

Thinking about how our actions strike emotional chords with parents (just as theirs do with us) can help us to be more sensitive.

❋ *"The teachers don't understand how my child feels!"*
It is hard for parents to see us looking so matter-of-fact when their children are miserable. If parents are from a different culture than the teacher, there may be a difference in accepted ways to express feelings.

❋ *"Why was my child placed in the less desirable classroom?"*
Sometimes parents get the mistaken (or sometimes accurate) impression that coveted placements with the favorite teacher or classroom go to favored families. If this is not the case, help parents understand how the placement process works.

❋ *"What happened to make my daughter unhappy at school?"*
Parents naturally look for a reason why a child, who previously came to school willingly, starts to resist. Even if parents have built a trusting relationship with last year's teacher, they are starting fresh with you.

Solving the Problem

To help parents move beyond their desire for a quick fix by moving their child to the other class, take steps to help them work through the transition.

※ *Listen to parents' concerns.*
Use language to let them know you hear them and understand how they feel. Don't try to defend the placement decision. "You were really surprised when Tanya had another rough transition. You expected that was all behind you. Tanya says she is sad because she isn't with her friends."

※ *Share information about how placement decisions were made.*
"We wanted Tanya to be in this class because we thought it would be a good match for her. My teaching assistant plays the Autoharp, and we know how much Tanya loves music. We thought she would enjoy playing with some of the children who weren't in her class last year."

※ *Let the parent know how Tanya is doing at school while acknowledging her experience.*
"After you leave, Tanya cries for a few minutes. She is willing to sit in my lap and accepts comfort from me. Yesterday, I asked her if she wanted to draw a picture for you, which really made her feel better. I'm glad you told me how she is feeling so I know she needs a little more support in making friends."

※ *Tell the parent what you expect.*
The parent only knows what she is experiencing right now. "I have seen other children go through a few weeks of missing their old class and old friends. I expect in a couple of weeks she will be very comfortable and won't long for the other class."

※ *Tell the parent which steps you will take to help their child make the transition.*
Parents can be reassured when a concrete plan is in place.

※ *Let the parent know how she can help.*
"If you can learn the names of the other children in our class, you can ask Tanya about them. I wouldn't ask if they are her friends, she may feel pressured to create instant friends. If you ask her, 'What did Alice wear today?' or 'What did Antonio bring for lunch?' she will have a reason to pay attention to the other children, which is a first step toward friendship."

※ *Tell the parent why her child will benefit from staying in your class.*
"I'm afraid if we move Tanya to the other class now, she will miss the opportunity to make a comfortable transition to a new class. She will have lots of changes in her life, and we can give her support to build

confidence in preschool. I really feel that she will be happy in this class once she's made the adjustment."

❊ *Ask the parent to give it time to work.*
If a month from now the child is still miserable, more may be going on.

❊ *Communicate often with the parent during the transition period.*
Simple e-mails or phone calls let the parents know that you are still thinking about Tanya's needs.

After the Problem Is Solved: Moving Toward True Partnership

How do you involve families in the enrollment process? Even if you don't want to let it turn into a popularity contest, you can ask parents what they think their children need in a classroom or a teacher. Learn this information by using questionnaires or having personal conversations.

Before You Have a Problem

Read through the following list and check off what you have already accomplished (see pages 89–93). If many of the checkboxes are blank, you have work to do to create an environment where problems are easy to solve.

☐ *Offer parents information about development and resources for learning more.*
Prepare parents for the beginning of a new year and for potential problems adjusting. We tend to give the issue a lot of energy when children first enter a program and forget that it will continue to be an issue.

☐ *Share information with parents about child guidance.*
Give parents tips for preparing children for a new class. If rosters are available beforehand, let parents know who will be in the same class with their children so they can work on those connections as soon as possible.

☐ *Remember that there is more than one right way to work with children.*
Listen to what parents tell you about their child's friendship patterns. Just because it may work for you most of the time to move children into new groups, maybe parents know something that could help you make that decision.

• •

Scenario 4: The Child Who Can Do No Wrong, or, "Not my baby!"

Nicky's teacher paints a picture:

"Nicky is one of those kids I always have to keep an eye on. He doesn't have a lot of impulse control. He pinches other kids or knocks them over, and then looks innocent. I tried to talk to his mom about it. She just can't accept that he isn't an angel. She makes excuses for him or insists that I must have missed what the other child did to him first. She is making his behavior worse!"

Nicky's mom says:

"I don't think Nicky's teacher likes him. She is always blaming him for things. He's just a little boy! Sometimes when he really likes another child he is a little too affectionate and doesn't know his own strength. He really is sweet."

What Is the Problem?

Acknowledging their children's misbehavior can be difficult for parents. One of the issues is the expectation of parents who are not keeping up with their child's development. When parents learn to care for their newborn, they are told that their child isn't crying to get attention; the baby is letting his needs be known. As children move from unintentional actions to intentional actions, parents may not make the transition.

It can also be difficult to watch the child you love behave in ways that aren't loveable or to accept the child's negative emotions.

What Are You Thinking?

Be aware of how your reaction might make the situation worse. It is easier to move into finding positive solutions if you can avoid getting into the following mind-sets, recognizing them as unhelpful to developing a healthy partnership with parents. Typical defensive reactions include these:

☀ *"The parents are spoiling that child!"*
It can be hard to watch parents miss opportunities to teach their children responsibility, but teachers have no control over this. While we can provide insight to parents who are ready to hear it, we must ultimately let go.

☀ *"Other children and parents will lose respect for my authority if I can't get this child to behave."*
Your ego is not what counts in these situations. What is good for children is what matters. Rise above your concern for appearance and do what you know is right.

What Are Parents Thinking?

Thinking about how our actions strike emotional chords with parents (just as theirs do with us) can help us to be more sensitive.

☀ *"She doesn't understand my son."*
Parents will accept most things if they believe that you truly know their child and will act on his behalf.

☀ *"He is just a little child. What does the teacher expect?"*
Expectations vary by culture. Some cultures give children more time to not be responsible for their behavior.

☀ *"What does the teacher expect? He's all boy."*
A secondary issue is that in some cultures, expectations for boys are different from expectations for girls. If you know this to be the case, you can frame the behavioral expectations for the child in terms of what will be expected of him by peers of grade school teachers rather than making it a moral issue.

Solving the Problem

The best way to help the child change his behavior is to work with parents on a consistent message and reaction to misbehaviors.

☀ *Give parents honest information about their child.*
It is tempting to pretend that the child is behaving fine at school and to handle the issue without involving parents. Unless you have reason to believe that sharing information with the parent will place the child at risk for abuse, you must give parents accurate information. They may not be ready to hear it from you, but this child's kindergarten teacher may get through to them, and they'll realize it has been an issue all along.

☀ *Be prepared for a negative reaction from the parent.*
Avoid a negative reaction by offering concrete examples of the behavior you are addressing. Saying, "Nicky reached over to another child and took the cookie cutter out of his hand while the other child was yelling no," is specific. Saying, "Nicky always takes the other kids' toys," is not.

☀ *Don't get defensive.*
If the parent questions your judgment or the reliability of your observations, remember how defensive the parent feels and don't take it personally. Assume that the parent is also interested in seeing the child's behavior improve.

☀ *Work with the assumption that you and the parent have the same ultimate goal.*
You can make a parent defensive by asking if they allow their child to behave in a certain way. By starting off with the assumption that you have the same goal, you can establish a team with the parents.

☀ *Act with integrity.*
Don't talk about other children. If the parent baits you with observations about other children, firmly remind her that it is inappropriate to talk about other children. The purpose of the talk is to deal with her child.

☀ *Get help.*
If tensions are high, get an administrator to help you talk to the parent. I have watched parents bully staff into allowing unacceptable behavior from children to avoid confrontation. A third party can keep the conversation on topic.

☀ *Find common goals and actions you can both agree to.*
Focus on the behavior goal for the child, not the needs of the other children in the class. Parents will appreciate your desire to help their child learn prosocial behavior.

☀ *Meet parents on their turf.*
If you can interest the parents in working with you to change the child's behavior, give them the time and support for consistency between home and school. A home visit can provide insight for you and let the child know that expectations will be consistent between home and school.

☀ *Involve parents in the solution.*
You can keep a behavior log that goes between home and school.

After the Problem Is Solved: Moving Toward True Partnership

Rather than predetermining behavioral expectations, you can build them with the parents in the program. A parent meeting before school starts can be a time to set goals and expectations that everyone accepts.

Before You Have Problems

Read through the following list and check off what you have already accomplished (see pages 89–93). If many of the checkboxes are blank, you have work to do to create an environment where problems are easy to solve.

☐ *Keep in mind that development is dynamic.*
Children's development and behavior is influenced by the expectations of the adults they care for. Establish your fondness for the child before addressing behavioral issues. Parents will find it easier to listen to criticism from someone who cares.

☐ *Offer parents information about development and resources for learning more.*
Invite the parent to observe the classroom. Sometimes parents will see behavior without having it pointed out.

☐ *Share information with parents about child guidance.*
Have in writing a clear policy for discipline. Make sure parents understand it before school begins.

Discussion Questions

1. Did your parents have reasonable expectations of you as a child? Which of their expectations now seem too young or too old? Did they base their expectations on the advice of others (such as family members), their own memories of childhood, or "expert" advice from reading books, magazines, or taking parenting classes?
2. With what age of children do you feel most comfortable? What is it you like about this age? What abilities or behaviors do you want to avoid by not working with another age group?
3. Have you moved from working with one age group to another? If so, what were the surprises for you in what the new age group could or couldn't do?

References

Balaban, Nancy. 1985. *Starting school: From separation to independence: A guide for early childhood teachers*. New York: Teachers College Press.

Galinsky, Ellen. 1987. *The six stages of parenthood*. New York: Perseus Books.

Gonzales-Mena, Janet. 1995. *Dragon mom: Confessions of a child development expert*. Napa, Calif.: Tattle OK Publications.

Honig, Alice S. 2002. *Nurturing infant-toddler attachment in early care settings*. Washington, D.C.: NAEYC.

McCracken, Janet Brown. 1980. "So many goodbyes" (brochure). Washington, D.C.: NAEYC.

Neugebauer, Bonnie. 1992. *Alike and different: Exploring our humanity with young children*. Redmond, Wash.: Child Care Information Exchange.

———. 1994. Going a step further—No traditional holidays. *Child Care Information Exchange* 100.

Paley, Vivian Gussin. 1995. *You can't say you can't play*. New York: Teachers College Press.

Saifer, Steffan. 1997. *Practical solutions for practically every problem: The early childhood teacher's manual*. St. Paul: Redleaf Press.

Stonehouse, Anne. 1995. *How does it feel? Child care from a parent's perspective*. Redmond, Wash.: Child Care Information Exchange.

U.S. Department of Justice. 1997. *Commonly asked questions about child care centers and the Americans with Disabilities Act*. http://www.usdoj .gov.

Other Resources from Redleaf Press

MAGIC CAPES, AMAZING POWERS: TRANSFORMING SUPERHERO PLAY IN THE CLASSROOM

by Eric Hoffman

Magic Capes, Amazing Powers takes an in-depth look at why children are so strongly attracted to superhero and weapons play, as well as at the concerns of parents and teachers, and ultimately suggests practical solutions that take into account the needs of both children and adults.

TRANSITION MAGICIAN FOR FAMILIES: HELPING PARENTS AND CHILDREN WITH EVERYDAY ROUTINES

by Ruth Chvojicek, Mary Henthorne, and Nola Larson

Dozens of activity ideas for caregivers to share with families to simplify the everyday transitions outside of child care.

NO BITING: POLICY AND PRACTICE FOR TODDLER PROGRAMS

by Gretchen Kinnell for the Child Care Council of Onondaga County, Inc.

The "how-to" manual for every toddler program seeking to address biting incidents from developmental, emotional, and practical perspectives.

GOOD GOING! SUCCESSFUL POTTY TRAINING FOR CHILDREN IN CHILD CARE

by Gretchen Kinnell for the Child Care Council of Onondaga County, Inc.

Designed as a comprehensive approach to potty training in child care, *Good Going!* addresses the issues involved when children are potty trained in the classroom as well as in the home.

SO THIS IS NORMAL TOO? TEACHERS AND PARENTS WORKING OUT DEVELOPMENTAL ISSUES IN YOUNG CHILDREN

by Deborah Hewitt

Makes the challenging behaviors of children a vehicle for cooperation among adults and stepping stones to learning for children.

THE KINDNESS CURRICULUM: INTRODUCING YOUNG CHILDREN TO LOVING VALUES

by Judith Anne Rice

Create opportunities for kids to practice kindness, empathy, conflict resolution, and respect.

 800-423-8309
www.redleafpress.org